THE BEAN BOOK

Rose Elliot is one of Britain's most famous writers on vegetarian cookery. She is the author of many best-selling books and her original and imaginative style has made her a favourite among vegetarians and non-vegetarians alike. Her recipes range from creations of subtle sophistication to simple and cheap dishes for the novice cook and those on a tight budget.

Rose Elliot became a cookery writer by accident. She was planning to take a degree in history when she met and married her husband and became involved in cooking, entertaining and bringing up a family. For many years she has tried out all her recipes at home, the very best of which she has included in her books.

ROSE ELLIOT

The Bean Book

FONTANA/COLLINS

First published in Fontana 1979
Eleventh impression April 1988

Set in Monotype Garamond

Printed and bound in Great Britain by
William Collins Sons & Co. Ltd, Glasgow

Contents

Acknowledgements

My grateful thanks to all the people who have helped, encouraged and advised me: to D. Driscoll of Stevens and Brotherton Ltd, for information on varieties and origins of beans; to Brian Wilmot, of the US Dry Pea and Lentil Council and to the American Embassy in London for helpful information; to J. M. Dent and Co. Ltd for permission to quote from 'The Englishman' by G. K. Chesterton; to Dr Alan Long of the Research Section of the Vegetarian Society (UK) Ltd; and especially to my family, for eating beans at practically every meal while I was writing this book.

Preface

I'm an impulsive bean-buyer. When I go into a health shop or continental food store and see the dried beans and lentils, with their bright, shiny skins, varied shapes and sizes and beautiful colours, I find them irresistible. But I used to find that when I'd got them home they'd tend to linger over-long in the cupboard and every time I saw them there I'd feel rather guilty, particularly when I was constantly reading of their ecological value and how they can provide ten times as much protein as meat from a piece of land.

Thinking about the situation, I realized that the reason I didn't use the beans was because when I was unsure of their flavour and how long they'd take to cook it was easier to reach for the spaghetti and Parmesan. I thought that if I knew a bit more about the beans I'd be able to use them as quickly and easily as other foods. So I decided to do something about the situation and set myself the task of trying to find out as much as I could about beans, and this book is the result.

I looked at the nutritional value of beans and the best ways of cooking them; I tasted as many varieties as I could find. I looked at traditional bean recipes from other countries; I invented, tested and experimented and my family tried and commented on the results. In fact there were times when we felt like the man in the saying: 'Shake a Leicestershire man by his collar, and you shall hear the beans rattle in his belly.'

As well as some undeniably austere-tasting dishes, which, you'll be pleased to hear, did not make the pages of this book, we found many that were really delicious and these now feature regularly in my cookery repertoire. Lovely spicy dals from India, for instance; crisp, tasty rissoles; delectable pâtés and

9

bean salads, shiny with dressing and fragrant with herbs.
Delicate bean dishes from France, robust ones from Italy;
others from the Middle East, with more than a hint of olive
oil, lemon and garlic, full of earthy charm.

In fact I really got quite hooked on beans, especially when I
saw the effect they were having on my housekeeping budget. I
do hope you'll find the same and enjoy the recipes in this book.

Introduction

According to archaeologists, dried peas, beans and lentils were among the first crops to be cultivated by man, and evidence of the remains of peas and lentils has been found in various excavations. Peas recently uncovered on the border between Thailand and Burma have been carbon-dated at around 9750 BC; others have been found in a Stone Age cave in Hungary and in the mud of the lake dwellings in Switzerland, dating back to the Bronze Age, about 3000 BC, while lentils have been discovered in Egyptian tombs dating from about 2000 BC. Although our garden pea of today is unknown in the wild state, certain plants in Central Asia, the Middle East and North Africa are cross-fertile with modern cultivated ones and this leads to the belief that they originated in Central Asia, with secondary development in the other two places. It is thought that Aryans from the East later introduced dried peas to the pre-Christian Greeks and Romans and the latter brought them with them when they invaded Britain.

In the Middle East, lentils were certainly cultivated (probably from wild species that still grow in Turkey and other parts) by the ancient Egyptians, Hebrews, Greeks and Romans, and they are frequently mentioned in the Bible. According to Genesis 25:30-4 it was for a 'pottage of lentils' that Esau sold his birthright; in 2 Samuel 17:28 we read that David was brought 'beans, lentils and parched pulse', and in 2 Samuel 23:11 a piece of land is described as 'full of lentils'.

The ancient Egyptians grew broad beans and they believed variously that the beans contained dead men's souls, and were therefore unclean, and that they were the symbol of life and should thus be venerated and offered to the gods.

In Greece and Rome beans were used for casting votes when electing magistrates and other public officers. The beans were thrown into a helmet, white ones for 'pro' votes and coloured ones for 'con' votes. When Pythagoras forbade his disciples to have beans, he meant not that they should abstain from eating them, but that they should not take part in politics or 'love beans', that is, political office. The term 'beans' also meant sexual indulgence and when Aristotle told his disciples to 'abstain from beans', he was not referring to their dietary habits. These explanations perhaps enable us to read in a new light such statements as that of Robert Burton in his *Anatomy of Melancholy*:

> That which Pythagoras said to his scholars of old,
> may be forever applied to melancholy men,
> 'A fabis abstinete', eat no beans

and that of Donald Robert Perry Marquis in *The Almost Perfect State*: 'There will be no beans in the Almost Perfect State.'

During the feast of Saturnalia, Greek and Roman children would use beans for drawing lots to find out who would be 'king', and this association of beans with the feast of Christmas and the New Year can also be found in the old Western European custom of hiding a dried bean in a cake, the person getting this slice becoming 'king' of the revels. It is thought that originally the 'king' may have reigned for the whole of the twelve days of Christmas, his chief function being to perform the propitiatory rites to ensure good weather. In Italy lentils were traditionally eaten on New Year's Day to bring luck and good fortune during the coming year.

In the Middle Ages beans became associated with various spells and magic potions. For instance, it was believed that beans would cure baldness, and boiled beans mashed with garlic were taken for colds and coughs, a remedy not without virtue, according to modern herbalists, but on account of the garlic rather than the beans! Nicholas Culpepper (1616-54) mentions beans in his *British Herbal*, published in 1653, advising that 'bean flour is used in poultices to assuage inflammations rising upon wounds.' He goes on to list various troubles: 'felons, biles, bruises or blue marks by blows, or the imposthumes in the kernels of the ears', advising that beans 'helpeth them all'.

Before the end of the sixteenth century botanists in Belgium, Germany and England had written about and described many kinds of dry peas. But even a century later they were still a rare delicacy in France, fetching fantastic prices, though they later gained the reputation of being rather vulgar, as one seventeenth-century writer remarked: 'It is a frightful thing to see persons so sensual as to purchase and eat green peas'.

Green peas also became associated with courting, and there was an old saying: 'Winter for shoeing, peascod for wooing'. This may allude to the custom whereby girls would place a peascod containing nine peas on the door lintel, in the belief that the first man who passed under it would be their future husband. William Browne of Tavistock (1591-1643) also connected peas with wooing in *Britannica's Pastorals*, II, 3, where he says:

> The peascod greene oft with no little toyle
> He'd seeke for in the fattest, fertil'st soile,
> And rend it from the stalke and bring it to her
> And in her bosome for acceptance woo her.

It's amusing in view of the traditional link between peas, wooing and fertility, to reflect that it was through his work on peas in the garden of his Augustinian monastery at Brünn, in Austria, last century, that Gregor Johann Mendel laid the mathematical foundation for the modern science of genetics.

Many sayings involving beans and peas evolved over the years. From the late 1850s 'beans' has meant money (as in 'I haven't got a bean', etc.), but actually this meaning is derived from the French word 'bien', or something good. The terms 'old bean', meaning 'good friend, good old thing', and 'to spill the beans', or 'to give away a secret', crept into the language later, the latter expression being American, but anglicized by 1928. As far as I can discover, the first time the expression 'full of beans' was used was in *Handley Cross* by Robert Smith Surtees, published in 1843, in which the description 'full o' beans and benevolence' occurs in Chapter 7. Then there is the old saying, 'He knows how many beans make five'. The right response to this apparently is, 'Yes, but how many blue beans make five white ones?' and the correct answer is, 'Five, if peeled', to which one can only add a loud groan.

The word 'beans' is used in both French and English to mean 'punishment' or 'retaliation', as in the old saying, 'I'll give him beans', and the French proverb, 'S'il me donne des pois, je lui donnerai des feves' – 'if he gives me peas, I'll give him beans', or, in other words, 'tit for tat'. Kipling also used the expression 'give beans', meaning 'to defeat severely'.

Then there is the saying, 'as like as two peas in a pod', which was quoted by Lyly as long ago as 1597 in *Euphues*: 'as lyke as one pease is to another', and the old country belief that the perfume of bean flowers had an adverse effect on the brain:

Quand les feves sont en fleur,
Les fous sont en vigeur.
('When beans are in flower, fools are in full strength.')

At least two words in modern use owe their origin directly to pulses. When the lens was discovered it was so-called because it resembled a lentil in shape; and the jewellers' carat was named after the carat bean. Because of its uniform size, this bean, which grows on the east coast of Africa, was used by the natives as their standard for weighing gold. This standard was later adopted by the Indians and applied to the grading of all precious stones.

Although pulses have continued to play an important part in the diet of the poorer peoples of the world, in India, China and the Middle East, apart from wartime, when housewives were urged to serve more 'body-building' beans, in the more affluent West they have been neglected in favour of animal proteins, or simply grown as food for livestock. It's only in recent years, with worry about the increasing world population and food shortages, that these foods have begun to receive more serious attention.

Today India is probably the world's largest producer of lentils, with an estimated average production of 8,000,000 cwt, all for domestic consumption. Russia is another large producer of lentils, although exact figures are not available. Other countries which produce sizeable quantities of lentils are Turkey, Egypt, Ethiopia, Syria, Morocco, Spain, Argentina and Chile. China and Russia are thought to be the world's largest producers of dry peas and it is estimated that China, Russia and other communist countries represent more than three-quarters of the total world production.

The USA is the largest exporter of lentils and one of the world's largest exporters of dry peas, with Great Britain her biggest customer – rather ironical when you consider that it was from Britain that the USA obtained the first dry pea seeds! The dry pea and lentil industry in the USA is based on Idaho and Washington and they call themselves the 'dry pea and lentil capitals of the world', with Michigan the centre of the dry bean industry.

In the 1920s the USA was the largest importer of dry beans; today she is the largest exporter, and again Britain is one of the biggest customers, mainly on account of the 850 million cans of baked beans consumed every year. The Americans have achieved their success in the dry bean industry by studying the market, by developing new heavy-cropping varieties, by mechanizing their harvesting, grading and packing and by organizing many promotional activities. In Michigan they even have an annual Bean Fair, with free bean soup and a beauty contest to find the 'bean queen', who must be a daughter of a bean farmer.

It would be good if we could develop our own bean industry further. The baked-bean canners are very interested in the production of a haricot bean which can be grown successfully in this country, to save having to import; a bean with the right flavour has been developed, but it is thought that consumers would object to its colour – dark blue! The main problem in this country is to find varieties which will mature quickly enough in our cold summers, but experiments have been going on for many years at places such as Henry Doubleday Research Association, and I hope there will be continued development and successful results.

Growing and Harvesting Pulses

Pulses – dry peas, beans and lentils – belong to the *leguminosae* family, that large group which, according to the Penguin *Dictionary of British Natural History* by Richard and Maisie Fitter, are 'characterized by the seeds being carried in a pod (legume) and the highly distinctive five-petalled flowers'. Numbering some 14,000 species, the *leguminosae* family is one of the largest groups of flowering plants, and members of it can be found in most parts of the world.

Although they generally prefer a warm, temperate climate, pulses will grow under very varied climatic and soil conditions and they, like other members of the *leguminosae* family, have the useful habit of being 'nitrogen fixing', which means that they leave the soil richer than they found it.

The lentil plant, *Lens esculenta*, can be found in Europe, Asia, the Middle East, North Africa and the USA. It has a bushy growth, normally attaining a height of between 1 and 1½ feet (30-45 cm). The leaves are made up of many oval leaflets that end in tendrils and the flowers are small and white or blue. They ripen into short, flat pods which are borne at the end of the branches, and each contains two seeds (lentils). The crop yield varies a good deal, but in the USA yields of 1500 and 1600 pounds an acre are not uncommon in favourable conditions.

The plants of dry peas, *Pisum sativum*, have a more climbing habit, normally reaching a height of about 30 or 36 inches (75-90 cm), although there is a winter variety which can reach 10 feet (300 cm), but this is grown only for green manure. The leaves consist of between two and six leaflets with the terminal ones modified into tendrils and the flowers are white or purplish, self-fertile and for the most part self-pollinating. The

17

seeds of commercial dry peas are round and smooth and there are between seven and nine peas in the pods which are much larger and fatter than those of the lentil plant.

There are many varieties of bean: of the common bean (*Phaseolus vulgaris*) alone there are 200 types and 400-500 named species. This is the kidney bean group and includes string and wax beans, haricot beans and the butter bean. The plants have a bushy habit, the leaves are usually composed of three pointed leaflets and the flowers are whitish, yellowish or purplish. Other important types of bean are the broad bean (*Vicia faba*), the Lima bean (*Phaseolus limensis*), the soya bean (*Glycine max*), the cow pea (*Vigna sinensis*), the mung, golden or green gram (*Phaseolus aureus*) and the adzuki bean (*Phaseolus angularis*).

There are, incidentally, other plants which are commonly referred to as beans but which are not. The castor bean, for instance, is a member of the spurge family, and the coffee bean is the seed of the coffee tree. The so-called sacred bean is the seed of the East Indian lotus plant, and the Mexican jumping bean is the seed of various trees in the spurge family. The seed becomes inhabited by the larva of a moth and as the larva moves the seed appears to jump!

All the pulses need a firm, fine seedbed and their normal growing season is about 90 days. In very dry areas the plants are allowed to dry completely before being harvested, but in damper conditions they are cut to encourage thorough drying before being harvested. In mechanical harvesting, the plants are passed through threshing cylinders which separate the pods from the vines, which are then ejected from the harvester as chaff.

The pulses pass through a number of processes during which the pods are removed and the seeds cleaned and graded. In the case of split peas, the seeds are soaked, steamed and tempered to loosen the fibrous outer seed coat, then the peas are bombarded against baffles in a splitter, which causes them to split in half through the cotyledons. After this each pea is graded, steamed and polished to produce the familiar shiny 'split peas' which we buy in the shops.

Nutritional Value

It's only in recent years that we've come to realize the full nutritional value of pulses. They used to be dismissed as 'second-class protein', and even in wartime advertisements, when the government wanted to encourage their use, they were said to be 'body-builders, though not quite as good as fish', while fish was only described as being 'practically equal to meat', which put the beans quite a long way down the scale! However, since then our understanding of protein has changed and we no longer think of protein as being 'first class' or 'second class'. We now know that there are different types of protein, and that if you put these different types together they complement each other to give full nutritional value. While pulse protein is valuable in its own right, it can be made all the more so by putting it with protein from another group. These other groups which complement pulse protein are:

> *cereal protein*, including rice, barley, millet and wheat, as in flour, bread and pasta, as well as the more unusual (to this country) forms such as bulgur and cracked wheat;
> *seed and nut protein*, particularly sesame seeds and sesame cream (tahini); also sunflower seeds and cashew nuts;
> *dairy protein*, eggs, milk – whole and skimmed – and milk products, such as hard cheese, cottage and curd cheese and yoghurt.

Although mixing proteins may sound daunting and complicated, it is in fact natural and almost instinctive. For instance, baked beans are usually served on toast, and it's very natural to serve lentil soup with bread, in both cases bringing together complementary proteins. I think it is interesting how many traditional peasant pulse dishes provide this complementary balance of protein. Indian dals, for instance, are made from pulses and are nearly always served with rice or a chapati made from wheat. Even nature seems to encourage this, too, because, agriculturalists tell me, rice and legumes are excellent crops to follow each other in rotation! The mixture of cereal and pulse protein is found in a number of traditional Italian recipes such as the popular *tuoni e lampo*, or 'thunder and lightning', in which chick peas are served with vermicelli, and in the Middle Eastern felafel, or little chick pea rissoles, which are eaten with Arab bread. It's interesting, too, that in both the Middle East and India, where so many pulses are eaten, yoghurt, another food which complements pulse protein, is extremely popular. But I think perhaps the most fascinating example of the natural blending of complementary proteins in a peasant dish is hummus, that creamy dip of puréed chick peas and tahini, or sesame cream, which is enjoyed throughout the Middle East.

Some people I know avoid serving pulses because they share the sentiment expressed in Edward Lear's limerick:

> There was an old person of Dean,
> Who dined on one pea and one bean;
> For he said. 'More than that,
> Would make me too fat,'
> That cautious old person of Dean.

One Hundred Nonsense Pictures and Rhymes

This caution is somewhat misplaced, however, especially if pulses are being served as a main course. According to *The Composition of Foods* by McCance and Widdowson, they contain only about 80 calories per ounce (28 g) dry weight, and four ounces (125 g) provide an ample course for anyone, with only half or a third of that quantity needed if they're being served alongside other protein. And as well as containing protein, they're a good source of iron, phosphorus and B vitamins.

Apart from being a good source of cheap protein, pulses are a particularly useful addition to our diet for two other reasons. First, they have the lowest fat content of any of the protein foods, and secondly their roughage or fibre content is extremely high; both important factors from the health point of view. Dr Andrew Stanway puts forward the case for a high fibre diet in his book *Taking the Rough with the Smooth* and recommends the inclusion in the diet of pulses, which he says are 'some of the richest sources [of fibre] of all . . . these can have up to 81 g of fibre per 1000 Kcals of energy supplied'. This is particularly impressive when you realize that other important protein foods – milk, eggs, fish and meat – contain no fibre at all. So it probably won't be just your purse which will benefit from the inclusion of more pulse-based meals in your diet!

Types of Pulse Available

ADZUKI BEANS

These are small, reddish-brown beans, rounded in shape with a point at one end. They have a strong, nutty, sweet flavour, and are much used in the macrobiotic diet, because, as Eunice Farmilañt says in *Macrobiotic Cooking*, they are 'the most yang beans'. They probably originate from China, and are imported from China and Thailand where they are harvested in November and December. In the Orient, adzuki beans are usually cooked to a rather soft consistency and served with such ingredients as coconut milk. They are also cooked with rice, their bright colour tinting the rice an attractive pink, as in the Japanese dish, Red-cooked Festival Rice. In the East it's also common to find adzuki beans sweetened with sugar and made into cakes and sweetmeats.

BLACK BEANS

One of the many members of the kidney bean family, black beans are large and shiny and much used in Caribbean cookery. One popular black bean dish from Cuba is called 'Moors and Christians', and consists of black beans cooked with rice and spices, black against white.

Black beans are mainly imported from Thailand, where they

are harvested in November and December. Like all the kidney beans, they cook to a deliciously succulent texture and are particularly attractive when mixed with other beans to give colour contrast in casseroles and salads. You can substitute black beans for red kidney beans in any of the recipes.

BLACK EYED BEANS

Sometimes referred to as black eyed peas, or cow peas, black eyed beans are a variety of cow pea. They are smaller than black beans, creamy coloured and kidney shaped, with a distinctive black spot or 'eye' on them, hence their name. They are thought to originate from Africa, but are now cultivated in many tropical countries and particularly in the southern USA, where they are sometimes grown as a hay crop. The plant has two forms: there is a short, erect variety, which is the one grown in the USA and harvested in September/October, and a climbing variety which is grown in China. We mainly import them from California.

Black eyed beans are one of the quicker cooking pulses and have a pleasant, savoury flavour and succulent texture. They can be used as a substitute for haricot or butter beans if you find these indigestible.

BORLOTTI BEANS

These beans are variously known as borlotti, borletti, salugia, crab-eye and rose cocoa beans. They are kidney shaped and range in colour from a pale, creamy pink to a deep, brownish pink, and are attractively speckled. The best are the pale ones. When cooked, they have a tender, moist texture and a sweetish, very pleasant flavour. They are imported from Italy, East Africa, Taiwan and Spain, the harvest generally being gathered in September and October.

Borlotti beans belong to the kidney bean family and can be used in any recipe in place of kidney or haricot beans for a change.

BRITISH FIELD BEANS

These are the ones which can be grown in gardens and allotments in this country. Types grown extensively here are the tic and daffa beans, and varieties of the broad bean which produce about 30 cwt an acre. The field beans which you can buy and grow at present tend to be roundish in shape with a brown skin. They are quite tasty, although the skin is rather tough and obtrusive, and so I think they are best made into soups, when they can be liquidized and sieved, or else cooked and passed through a vegetable mill before being mixed with other ingredients.

BROAD BEANS

Familiar to most gardeners, broad beans are flat and kidney shaped, with a hard, brownish skin. The skin is tough, like that of the British field bean, and so needs to be removed before the beans are served, although sometimes these beans can be bought (more expensively) skinned. The broad bean grows in many countries all over the world, supplies for this country being mainly imported from Spain, where they are harvested in August and September. They're not always easy to obtain – try Greek provision stores.

BUTTER BEANS

Probably the best known bean in Britain, butter beans come from Madagascar, where they are harvested in November and December. They are one of the largest beans, flattish, kidney shaped and creamy white in colour. I find them very useful; they can be served simply as a vegetable or part of a salad but are particularly good in curries, casseroles, pies and hotpots. They need careful cooking so that they are tender but not mushy.

CANNELLINI BEANS

Sometimes called fazolia beans, cannellini beans look like small white kidney beans, and indeed are a member of that family and can be used in any recipe calling for ordinary white haricot beans. They originate from Argentina but are widely grown in Italy from where we import them. The harvesting season is September/October.

CHICK PEAS

Sometimes called 'garbanzos', and native to Asia, chick peas are a great favourite in Middle Eastern and Mediterranean cookery, as well as in India, where they are known as 'gram'. In appearance chick peas look like rather small, dry hazel nuts and are light golden brown in colour. They retain their shape well when cooked and have a particularly appetizing aroma and taste; I think they are one of the most useful and delicious pulses. They are mainly imported from Morocco and Turkey, where they are harvested in August and September.

CONTINENTAL LENTILS

Another very useful and delicious pulse, with a strong, almost 'earthy' flavour. They are sometimes called 'green lentils' or 'brown lentils' and, indeed, can be grey, green, yellow or reddish brown in colour! Unlike split red lentils and split peas, continental lentils retain their shape after cooking and are therefore useful when you want to give textural interest to a dish. Popular in the Middle East, continental lentils are grown in many countries of the world, including Russia, India and the USA, but they are mainly imported to Britain from Spain, Argentina, the Lebanon and Chile, where they are harvested in May and June.

FLAGEOLET BEANS

Flageolet beans are pale green in colour and long and slim in shape. They are in fact haricot beans which have been removed from the pod while still young and tender, which accounts for their delicate green colour, tender texture – and high price! But although something of an extravagance, they make a very pretty salad for a special occasion and are also a particularly attractive addition to any bean mixture, because of their unusual colour.

These beans are grown in France and Italy, but main imports to this country come from the Argentine, where they are harvested in May and June, and Taiwan, where they mature in November and December. They're not as easy to find as some of the other beans; try health shops.

The name flageolet, incidentally, relates to the fact that the French thought they looked like a flute, or *flageolet*.

FUL MEDAMES BEANS

These beans, which come from Egypt, are smallish, round in shape and brown in colour. They have rather a tough outer skin and so need careful cooking, but when they are soft they have a pleasant, 'earthy' flavour. They are very popular in the Middle East, where, flavoured with garlic, olive oil and lemon juice, they can be served at any meal of the day, including breakfast! Try specialist Middle Eastern shops.

HARICOT BEANS

Small and oval in shape, creamy white in colour, haricot beans are a variety of kidney bean and are familiar to most people. They originate from Central and South America, being brought to Europe in the sixteenth century. They became known as haricot beans because the French included them in their stews or *haricots*. In the USA they are known as 'navy beans', a name apparently coined by Commodore Perry whilst eating them one day in Lake Erie during a British assault.

Although they're probably best known in Britain in the form of 'baked beans', haricot beans can be prepared in many delicious ways and are one of the most useful and easily obtainable of the pulses. They are mainly imported from the USA, Canada, Ethiopia, Chile, East Africa and the Sudan, their harvesting season being September and October.

LIMA BEANS

Native to tropical America, and called Lima because that is where the original seeds came from, these beans are sometimes called 'the aristocrat of the bean family'. They are rather like butter beans in appearance and are indeed referred to as butter beans in the southern USA. They have a lovely sweet flavour on account of their high sugar content. Unfortunately they are not easy to obtain in this country.

MUNG BEANS

Probably best known in this country in their sprouted form, as bean sprouts, mung beans are small, round and green and can be cooked like any other pulse. In fact they are one of the quicker cooking pulses and have a rather sweet flavour and soft texture. They can be cooked without soaking.

Native to India, mung beans are grown throughout Africa, China, the USA and India itself, where they are known as *mung dal*. They are mainly imported to this country from Australia, where they are harvested in May and June, and from Thailand and China, where their harvesting season is November and December.

PEAS

Looking like pale, wizened versions of fresh peas, dried peas, or 'soup peas' as they are called in the USA, cook to the familiar 'mushy peas' of school days, but, imaginatively cooked, they can be quite tasty, with their pleasant sweet flavour. Although they can be grown in this country, those found in the shops are likely to have been imported, probably from the USA and Canada, where they are harvested in August and September.

PINTO BEANS

Pinto beans are medium-sized and look rather like borlotti beans, with brown specks; in fact pinto means 'speckled'. They are yet another variety of the kidney bean and have a delicious savoury flavour and pink colour when they're cooked. They are used a lot in the USA, from where we import them, and their harvesting season is September and October.

RED KIDNEY BEANS

Rich red in colour and with the characteristic kidney shape, red kidney beans are one of the most attractive, both to look at and to eat. They cook to a deliciously 'mealy' texture and are excellent both in salads and substantial dishes. They are much used in South American and Caribbean cookery and also in that of India, where they are known as *rajma dal*. We import them largely from East Africa, the USA and Canada, where they are harvested in September and October.

SPLIT RED LENTILS

Sometimes referred to as 'Egyptian lentils', split red lentils are the bright orange-red ones which can be obtained from most supermarkets. Split red lentils are cultivated, in one or another variety, in the Middle East, in North Africa, in Europe, along the Mediterranean coast and as far north as Germany, the Netherlands and France. In the Middle East they have the reputation of being the best food to carry on long journeys.

Split red lentils cook quickly to a light golden beige and they do not need to be soaked first, although this does speed up their cooking time even more. They have a particularly pleasant, bland flavour, but they do not hold their shape, cooking to a soft mass. They are harvested in September and October and imported from Syria, Ethiopia and Nepal.

In Indian recipes, split red lentils can be used to replace *masur dal*, though botanists disagree as to whether or not these two are the same species.

SOYA BEANS

Originating in eastern Asia, and known and valued by the Chinese for thousands of years, soya beans have the highest protein content of any of the pulses and are small, round and yellowish-brown in colour. They are the hardest beans and, in their natural state, they need a long soak followed by several hours' cooking and then careful seasoning to make them palatable. However, a partially cooked variety known as soya 'splits' is available, and this cooks quickly (in about 30 minutes) without soaking.

Soya beans are also well known in their other form, as soya flour, which is soft, pale yellow and very rich in protein. The flour is useful for increasing the protein value of other foods, where this is a problem; it can also be used to make non-dairy milks and two types of 'cheese', which is useful for people who are allergic to these foods or who prefer not to eat dairy produce. One of the soya 'cheeses', bean curd, is widely used in Chinese cookery and can usually be bought, ready made, in shops specializing in Chinese foods or serving a large Chinese community.

Much experimental work is going into producing a variety of soya bean which will withstand the British summer and crop reliably. At present we mainly import soya beans from Canada, where they are harvested in September and October.

SPLIT PEAS

These, as their name suggests, are peas which have been split in half, their outer skin having been removed. Both yellow and green varieties are available, although the latter are not so easy to find.

Split peas have a pleasant, slightly sweet flavour, but, like split red lentils, do not hold their shape, disintegrating as they soften. They are harvested in August and September, yellow split peas being mainly imported from Canada, Hungary and the USA, green split peas coming from Canada and the USA.

Buying and Storing Pulses

It's pleasant buying pulses because they're so attractive, with their shiny appearance and bright colours. Lovely, too, to find an ever-increasing variety becoming available in health and wholefood shops, although it would be nice if more supermarkets and groceries would stock a wider range than the usual butter beans, haricot beans, split red lentils and yellow split peas. Perhaps a little consumer pressure might encourage them to add to their stock some of the more useful of the less well known ones, such as chick peas, which I always seem to be having to make a special journey to buy, or red kidney beans (often, unfortunately, available only in tins – a much more expensive way of buying them), and the delicious continental lentils. However, all these, and many of the others mentioned in this book, can usually be obtained from health shops; and if you have an Oriental, Indian, Mediterranean or Middle Eastern food shop near you, this is also a good place to look for some of the more unusual ones.

Although dried beans, peas and lentils are easy-going in that they can be stored on the shelf and do not perish easily, it is a mistake to think that they can be left at the back of the larder for months and months. Long storage can harden them to the extent that no amount of cooking will make them tender. For this reason, it is best to buy them in fairly small quantities, from a shop with a quick turnover, as you need them. If you do get landed with some dry old beans, children love them for sticking on to paper to make colourful collages, or as a filling for rattles and other assorted musical instruments. And if you like to weigh down a pastry flan case with dry beans when baking 'blind', you can save them for that, although personally I think all that business with bits of greaseproof paper and baking beans is a waste of time: simply pricking the base of the flan before cooking seems to be just as good.

Equipment

The equipment needed for pulse cookery is really simple and straightforward, and you probably already have everything you need in your kitchen. You need a large sieve in which to put the pulses when washing and rinsing them; a large china or glass bowl in which to soak them, and a medium-large heavy-based saucepan for cooking them in. I think the heavy cast-iron casseroles, which can be used either on top of the cooker or in the oven, are ideal for pulses. One or two of these in different sizes, plus a 1½ pint (850 ml) and a 3 pint (1.7 l) shallow oblong ovenproof dish should cater for most needs.

If you want to sprout beans and use them for making stir-fried Oriental mixtures, you'll find a *wok* very useful, although a large frying pan or saucepan will do instead. A pressure cooker is very useful because pulses take a minimum of 20-30 minutes and usually nearer an hour or more to cook, and a pressure cooker can reduce this by about two-thirds. A little care and experimentation is necessary, though, because it's quite easy to overcook some of the pulses, such as butter beans and black eyed beans, and reduce their lovely texture to a soft mush.

At the other end of the scale, one of those slow-cooking pots, which cooks food very gently for several hours on a small amount of electricity, is also excellent for cooking pulses, as is the old-fashioned, but just as effective, haybox.

Some of the pulses have rather obtrusive skins, and for this reason I think some form of food mill is useful for puréeing them. I use a mouli-légumes, which is quick and efficient and gives scope for textural variety with its choice of different plates. I also use a blender a good deal in pulse cookery, particularly for soups, and I also find I'm using it more and more to speed up other jobs, like making sauces, mayonnaise and pancake batter. I've given my quick blender recipes for these in the relevant sections in the book.

Dishes made from pulses have a homely quality about them, a comforting, rather earthy charm which can be enhanced by serving them simply, in chunky pottery. Presented attractively in this way and produced with a flourish – and certainly no apology – pulses have a very basic appeal, perhaps in view of the generations they've sustained, evoking archetypal memories, but certainly physically and aesthetically satisfying.

Preparation

Nicholas Culpepper, writing in the seventeenth century, called
beans 'extremely windy meat', an opinion which I know is
widely held today, and certainly discourages some people from
trying them. I have found, however, that the digestibility of
pulses depends to quite a large extent on how they are prepared
and cooked. When Culpepper goes on to say 'but if after the
Dutch fashion, when they are half boiled you husk them and
stew them (I cannot tell you how, for I never was a cook in all
my life) they are wholesome food,' I think he was on to something, because the secret seems to lie in rinsing – and sometimes parboiling and rinsing – the beans after they've been
soaked.

I asked Dr Alan Long of the Research Section of The
Vegetarian Society (UK) Ltd whether there was any scientific
basis for the 'indigestibility' of pulses and, if so, whether this
could really be modified by the method of preparation. This
was his reply:

Many cereals and pulses contain anti-nutritional factors
which are removed in processing, as in soaking, cooking,
fermenting or sprouting. Some pulses contain as many as
seven such factors. Some of these, such as cyanogenic sub-
stances (which decompose and liberate small amounts of
hydrocyanic acid or prussic acid, which are boiled off) are of
little concern in Western cuisines, but the enzyme inhibitors,
notably of the digestive enzyme trypsin, are important.
These are proteins, denatured, or otherwise inactivated, by
soaking, sprouting, fermenting or cooking.

Such processes, which operate faster on thin-skinned

beans and peas, also modify the starches, just as those in potatoes are made digestible. However, beans contain some unusual saccharides, notably raffinose, stachyose and verbascose, that may not be reduced in the fore-gut to metabolizable and absorbable sugars (as monosaccharides), so they enter the large intestine, where bacteria (which have prodigious powers of digestion) consume them, liberating carbon dioxide, hydrogen and methane (which are gases) and acetic and other acids. Evolution of these gases causes flatulence. It seems likely that we adapt in these ways to the pulse-saccharides:

1. We develop the required enzymic activity in the stomach and small intestine. This possibility seems remote, although we have adapted to life-long consumption of milk-sugar for which the 'natural' digestive system survives for only a few years after weaning;

2. The flora in the large intestine lack bacteria capable of breaking down the stachyose, etc., so they pass out unchanged;

3. The large intestines of people who can digest pulses contain bacteria which convert the saccharides into mainly non-gaseous metabolites (e.g. generating propionic rather than acetic acid). There are certainly genetic differences in people's reactions to the components in beans. The metabolism of ruminants can be altered in this way.

4. Social customs allow unexceptionable relief of wind, thus reducing pressure and discomfort in the sigmoid colon. The horse avails itself effectively of this ability.

The gastric motility induced by beans probably represents a beneficial effect, especially as so many people's diets lack in fibre. Anyway, you can be sure your culinary tricks with beans represent good nutritional sense.

In view of what Dr Long says, if you have trouble digesting pulses, I think it would certainly be worth taking extra care with the preparation, and possibly concentrating on the thinner-skinned varieties – you can tell which these are by

looking at the table of cooking times on pages 43–4; the thinner
the skin, the more quickly they cook.

Anyway, here's the method of preparation that I've found
works; basically it consists of four processes: washing, soaking,
rinsing and cooking, with an optional extra parboiling-and-
rinsing before the final cooking if you find it's necessary to make
them digestible for you.

WASHING

Pulses may be in greater or lesser need of washing depending
on how and where they were bought. Obviously those bought
from an old sack or barrel in a grain shop need it more than the
polythene-packed ones from the supermarket, although I like
to swish some cold water through even these. If the pulses look
very dusty, I think it's best to put them first into a bowl of
cold water, swirl them round well and check for any foreign
bodies such as the odd bit of stick or stone. Then put them into
a large sieve and run some cold water through them, moving
them around with your fingers to make sure that the water gets
to them all. Cleaner pulses can just be rinsed in the sieve.

SOAKING

There's no doubt that most pulses benefit from an initial
soaking before cooking. This not only speeds up the subse-
quent cooking time but also helps to make them more digestible. There are two ways of soaking pulses:

1. *The long cold soak*, which means covering the pulses with

twice their volume in cold water and leaving them to soak for 4-8 hours, or overnight.

2. *The short hot soak*, which is a boon if you've forgotten to get organized in advance! For this method, you simply put the washed pulses into a saucepan, cover them with plenty of cold water, and bring them to the boil. Let them boil vigorously for 2-3 minutes, then remove them from the heat, cover the saucepan and leave them to soak for 45-60 minutes.

RINSING

After they've soaked, it helps to make the pulses more digestible if you then put them into a large sieve and rinse them thoroughly under cold, running water, to wash away some of those 'unusual saccharides' which Dr Long mentioned. And if you're really worried about digestibility, follow this process by the additional parboiling-and-rinsing: put the pulses into a saucepan, cover them with cold water and boil them for 5 minutes, then turn them into a colander and rinse them again under cold, running water.

COOKING

Put the pulses into a saucepan or casserole and cover them generously with water or stock. Flavourings can be added, but don't put in any salt, as this toughens the outside of the beans and prevents them from cooking properly. For this reason, if you're using stock for cooking the beans, make sure that it isn't a salty one; see page 61. Acids, such as vinegar and lemon juice, and also tomatoes, have a similar effect on pulses, so are best added after the initial cooking, although I have found that tomatoes are all right with the quick-cooking pulses in small quantities, or if there is plenty of stock to dilute the acid.

Never add bicarbonate of soda to pulses; while this may be helpful in that it speeds up the cooking time, it is disastrous from the point of view of the flavour and nutritional value of the pulses.

Pulses can be cooked on top of the cooker or in the oven. Obviously it is not worth heating the oven specially, but if it's on to cook something else, such as a fruit cake or casserole, it's a good idea to make use of the heat to cook some pulses, which can simmer away quietly, without any fuss, towards the bottom of the oven.

PRESSURE COOKING

Use 15 lb per cubic inch pressure and cook the pulses for about a third of the time given. As the time pulses take to cook can vary, I find, from batch to batch, it's probably best to look at them a little before you think they should be done, to make sure.

Some of the pulses, particularly the split red lentils and split peas, tend to 'froth up' when they come to the boil, and this can clog the valve of the pressure cooker. To avoid this, just add a couple of tablespoons of oil to the cooking water.

USING A SLOW COOKER

It's best to follow the manufacturers' instructions for this, but basically you just put the pulses into the casserole, cover them with water (which can be hot or cold), put the lid on, and leave them to cook. The cooking time varies according to the type of pulse, the amount you're using, whether you put in hot or cold water and the temperature setting, but as a rough guide, starting from cold, with the temperature set at 'high', split red lentils take about 1 hour, butter beans 4-5 hours.

RED KIDNEY BEANS – A WARNING

You may have heard that, under certain conditions, it can be dangerous to eat red kidney beans. The toxic factor is most probably a haemagglutinin which may lead to acute gastroenteritis if not destroyed by adequate cooking. Soaking and rinsing the beans prior to cooking reduces the haemagglutinins by two thirds (to about the level present in other dried beans, soaked or unsoaked). The danger can be eliminated entirely by *ensuring that the beans are allowed to boil vigorously for 10 minutes* before lowering the heat and letting the beans cook gently until tender. It is safe to use a slow cooker *provided they are boiled for 10 minutes* as above, before being put into the slow cooker.

STORING COOKED PULSES

Cooked pulses will keep for several days in a covered container in the refrigerator and they also freeze well. I find it worthwhile cooking a double batch, using half and storing the rest in either the refrigerator or freezer, ready for another meal. This saves time, effort and fuel, particularly with the slower-cooking pulses. On the other hand, I think that to keep large stocks of ready-cooked beans in the deep freeze would be somehow to miss the point of them when they keep so well in their dried state!

Incidentally, most of the dishes in this book, including pulse soups and salads (apart from fresh garnishes like parsley and lettuce leaves, of course), will freeze beautifully after cooking. Except for little croquettes and rissoles, which can be fried from frozen, I find it best to let them thaw out completely before heating.

Cooking Times

As I've already mentioned, pulses seem to vary a good deal from batch to batch, and so these cooking times should be regarded as approximate, but I hope they will be useful as a rough guide.

ADZUKI BEANS	30 minutes
BLACK BEANS	1 hour
BLACK EYED BEANS	30-45 minutes
BORLOTTI BEANS	1 hour
BRITISH FIELD BEANS	30 minutes
BROAD BEANS	1½ hours
BUTTER BEANS	1¼ hours
CANNELLINI BEANS	1 hour
CHICK PEAS	1-1½ hours
CONTINENTAL LENTILS, SOAKED	30-45 minutes
UNSOAKED	1-1¼ hours
FUL MEDAMES BEANS	1 hour
HARICOT BEANS	1-1½ hours
KIDNEY BEANS	1 hour
LIMA BEANS	45-60 minutes
MUNG BEANS, SOAKED	20-30 minutes
UNSOAKED	30-40 minutes
PEAS	45 minutes
PINTO BEANS	1-1¼ hours

RED SPLIT LENTILS, SOAKED	15-20 minutes
UNSOAKED	20-30 minutes
SOYA BEANS	3-4 hours
SPLIT PEAS, SOAKED	30 minutes
UNSOAKED	40-45 minutes

Additional Ingredients

Pulses are one of the most basic of foods and are simple to prepare and cook, but the skill comes in the flavouring and presentation. Anyone can dish up a bowl of plain butter beans, and very dull too. But cook the butter beans in olive oil with tender button mushrooms, coriander and lemon juice, serve them chilled with soft fresh bread, and you've got one of the most delicious starters there is. Or mix them with leeks, carrots, mushrooms and tomatoes, top with a crust of crisp golden flaky pastry and they make a really tasty family meal. This type of cookery takes a little longer than just putting a joint in the oven, but it is also curiously satisfying. After all, most people can get a good result with expensive foods, but producing something really mouth-watering from cheap, simple ingredients takes a special kind of flair and presents a particular challenge – and great satisfaction when you succeed.

Because they've mostly got a fairly bland taste, pulses give one a good deal of scope with additional flavouring. These are the ingredients which I find most useful in pulse cookery:

FATS

These go particularly well with pulses, giving them a lovely shiny coating if they're simply cooked and making them moist and delectable. Of the hard fats, I think it's well worth while using butter when possible, because the flavour goes so well with the pulses – simply adding a knob of butter, a squeeze of lemon juice and a grinding of black pepper to boiled beans makes all the difference.

For the same reason, I like to use olive oil when I can, particularly in bean salads, although I do quite often economize by mixing olive oil with a good quality blended vegetable oil.

An unusual fat which goes well with pulses is creamed coconut. This is a hard white fat which you can get at health shops and it gives the beans a delicate, sweetish flavour reminiscent of Caribbean cookery. It's used in the West Indian Red Beans recipe and is good added to bean curries. It will keep for several weeks in the refrigerator.

LIQUIDS

Here, too, flavour is important, and cooking the pulses in a tasty stock makes all the difference to the result, but beware of using too salty a stock for reasons already explained; if you haven't any stock available, good results can still be obtained by making up an unsalted one as described on page 61.

I must admit that I do think the addition of a little wine or cider really does wonders for a pulse dish. I find even a small quantity of these – one or two tablespoonfuls – really gives the dish a lift. I find the remains of a bottle of wine will keep well in the refrigerator for a long time; while one wouldn't want to drink it at this stage, it seems perfectly all right for flavouring purposes. A little sherry is often added to stir-fry bean sprout and bean curd dishes and this again really improves the flavour.

VEGETABLES

Strongly flavoured vegetables such as onions, leeks, garlic, celery, peppers, mushrooms and tomatoes go particularly well with pulses. Peel, trim and chop or slice as necessary, then either fry the vegetables in fat before adding the soaked and rinsed pulses, or cook the vegetables separately and mix them with the cooked pulses, according to the particular recipe. Tomatoes, which are acid, are best added after the pulses have been cooked, as explained on pages 40-1.

Another vegetable which is good with pulses is, perhaps surprisingly, spinach; a combination which is found in some of the oldest pulse recipes. Root vegetables – carrots, turnips, parsnips, swedes – blend well with pulses, too, producing warming, satisfying winter dishes. Again, the raw vegetables can be cooked with the pulses, after the latter have been soaked, rinsed and possibly parboiled, or the two can be cooked separately, depending on the recipe.

FRUIT

The sweet-acid quality of many fruits seems to go particularly well with pulses, and almost all pulses I find are enhanced by the addition of a squeeze of lemon juice after cooking, and perhaps a little of the grated rind, too. Cubes of pineapple, chopped cooking or dessert apple, dried fruits such as apricots, sultanas or raisins are also good, giving a Middle Eastern flavour, while rings of banana make a lovely garnish for a spicy lentil curry.

HERBS AND SPICES

These, perhaps more than anything, make all the difference to the appeal of the finished dish. It is surprising what the addition of a bouquet garni, or even just a bayleaf, to the cooking water of any of the pulses will do for the flavour. As well as the bouquet garni herbs – bay, thyme and parsley – other useful ones are marjoram, oregano, rosemary, sage and mint, all of which seem to have a certain affinity with pulses. Fennel, cumin, coriander, mustard and cardamom are also useful; crush them first if necessary, using a pestle and mortar or the back of a wooden spoon. Cinnamon and ginger are good, too; you can use ground ginger or the kind which is preserved in syrup, but the best of all is fresh root ginger, if you can get it. It looks like a piece of gnarled root (which is what it is, of course) and you simply peel it and then grate it finely. It gives a lovely flavour, quite unlike the other types of ginger. I find the unpeeled root keeps quite well in the salad container at the bottom of the refrigerator.

Another of my favourite flavourings for pulses is chilli powder, which can be used to give a dish a subtle 'lift' or a definitely hot and spicy flavour, according to taste. Also useful are cayenne pepper, paprika pepper, tabasco sauce, cloves, garam masala and turmeric. And of course salt (I personally like sea salt) and freshly ground black pepper are essential. The use of a monosodium glutamate (MSG) flavouring powder is common in Oriental cookery and I have suggested this in the stir-fried recipes, but you could omit this if you prefer, and season carefully with sea salt.

Chopped fresh green herbs are lovely for garnishing pulse soups and for adding flavour to bean salads. Parsley and chives, of course, and mint, but also basil, lovage, fennel, dill and tarragon, as available.

OTHER INGREDIENTS

Dairy products such as cream and yoghurt can be added to cooked pulses just before serving, and go well with them, particularly the latter. If the pulses are being formed into rissoles, sometimes an egg is added for binding, and grated cheese also goes well with most of the pulses. I especially like hardboiled eggs with pulses, particularly continental lentils, and mayonnaise goes well with some pulse dishes, such as lentil loaves and cutlets when they're served cold.

Cooked rice and pasta are also very good with pulses and often feature with them in Mediterranean, Middle and Far Eastern dishes.

Garnishes such as triangles of crisp toast or fried bread croûtons, crunchy raw onion rings, lemon wedges or chopped parsley do not take a moment to prepare and often add that final touch that makes all the difference to the appeal of the meal.

Sprouting Beans

Something totally different that you can do with beans – and any other whole pulse, for that matter – is to 'sprout' them. Basically this means keeping them in a damp condition for anything from 2-5 days and rinsing them off in cold water two or three times a day to remove toxins produced. The result will be beans which are soft enough to eat without cooking, with lovely crunchy 'sprouts' on them. Nutritionally they're very rich in vitamins A and C; according to Esther Munroe in *Sprouts*, 'one half cup of almost any sprouted seed provides as much vitamin C as six glasses of orange juice.' A handful of sprouts included in a salad or stir-fry vegetable mixture immediately increases its food value.

BEANS TO CHOOSE

Of course the classic beans to sprout are the little round green mung beans, which are the ones which produce the bean sprouts used in Chinese cookery. But you can use any other clean, good quality dried peas or beans; chick peas are particularly good, so are adzuki beans, which are the other ones which are 'sprouted' in the East, and whole lentils – but not split peas or lentils, of course.

PREPARATION

The beans increase enormously in volume when sprouted, so don't do too many at a time. Three rounded tablespoons of mung beans will produce two cupfuls of sprouts in 3-4 days. Wash the beans, cover them with cold water and leave them to soak overnight. Next day rinse them under cold running water. Now you've got a choice of two methods for preparing the beans.

THE JAR METHOD

This is probably the best known method of sprouting beans. You simply put the prepared beans or lentils into a clean jar, remembering they'll increase in volume about six times, and cover the top of the jar with a piece of muslin secured with an elastic band. You then put the jar in a warm, dark, dry place, remembering to rinse the beans two or three times a day by running cold water into the jar through the muslin, swilling it round to wash the beans, then pouring it out again, without removing the muslin. It's a good idea to leave the jar at an angle on the draining board for a while afterwards to make sure all the water drains away. Actually I generally keep the jar near the sink all the time, otherwise I tend to forget to rinse the sprouts, but I wrap a piece of brown paper round the jar to keep the light out so that the sprouts will be a nice white colour.

THE COLANDER METHOD

For this method you need a colander and two pieces of old towelling (which can be used and re-used). You line the colander with a $\frac{1}{2}$ inch (1 cm) layer of towelling and wet it thoroughly with cold water. Lay your pre-soaked beans on the towelling in a single layer, then cover them with another $\frac{1}{2}$ inch (1 cm) layer of wet towelling. Make sure the whole thing is nice and damp, then set the colander over a bowl so that any excess water can drain away. Rinse the pulses three times a day by putting the colander under the cold tap. There's no need to disturb the beans or the towelling in order to do this. Then set them over the bowl again to drain.

USING THE BEAN SPROUTS

When the bean sprouts are ready, turn them out of the jar or colander into a bowl of fresh cold water and swish them around to wash them and loosen and rinse off the outer seed coats. Then drain them and use as required. They will keep in a plastic container in the bottom of the refrigerator for several days. Personally, I don't think there's any need to remove the sprouts from the beans before use as they add nourishment and give a lovely crunchy texture.

Making Bean Curd

Soya beans are probably most widely eaten in the form of bean curd, or *tofu*, which is included in many Chinese and Japanese recipes. It can be bought canned or fresh from Oriental grocers and some delicatessens and looks rather like a square of cream cheese. It will keep for a day or two in a container of water in the refrigerator and will also freeze. But it's quite easy to make your own bean curd at home: you need 8 oz (225 g) soya flour, 1½ pints (850 ml) cold water and the juice of 2 lemons.

Put the soya flour and water into a good-sized saucepan and simmer gently for 5 minutes, then stir in the lemon juice and ½ teaspoon sea salt and leave the mixture to cool (it will also thicken up). While this is happening, line a large sieve with a double layer of butter muslin or new, clean dishcloth material – there must be an overlap so that you can gather up the corners later. Set the sieve over a bowl. Pour the cooled soya mixture through the sieve, then gather up the muslin or dishcloth material and tie it; then suspend it in some convenient place, over a bowl, and leave it to drip for 8-12 hours. Once it has finished dripping, you can firm it up by placing a plate and a weight on top of it. Keep the bean curd in a plastic container in the refrigerator. These quantities make about 1 lb (450 g) of bean curd. I do not keep home-made bean curd in a container of water because I find it has a softer texture than the bought variety and is better just stored in a covered container.

Menu-planning with Pulses

> But since he stood for England
> And knew what England means,
> Unless you give him bacon,
> You must not give him beans.

So said G. K. Chesterton in 'The Englishman' and, indeed, that's what many people used to think. But, as I've already explained, beans without bacon are perfectly acceptable, even to Englishmen, and can certainly stand on their own as the main dish of the meal. But all the pulses are also versatile, being equally at home in soups, starters and salads, as well as substantial main dishes. This means that they offer considerable scope for creative menu-planning, particularly when used in conjunction with cereal, seed and dairy complementary proteins.

When planning menus, there's no need to stick rigidly to the pattern of serving the bulk of the protein in the main course. If you want to serve, say, a curry made from a colourful selection of vegetables but containing no protein, the answer is to start the meal with a tasty dal soup which will complement the rice which goes with the curry, and provide a beautifully balanced meal. Or, for a summer meal, you could have a chilled haricot bean and green herb salad served with warm rolls, followed by a well-flavoured ratatouille and buttery spinach, with cheese-cake or yoghurt for dessert. In this way you can get full value from your proteins, and really save money. Here are some other menu ideas based on recipes in this book:

LUNCHES

Aïgroissade with warm wholewheat rolls
Crisp lettuce
Fresh fruit

Beany salad bowl
Garlic bread
Cheese board
Fresh fruit

Felafel with Arab bread or soft wholewheat bread
Salad of lettuce, tomatoes, onion rings and black olives
Chilled yoghurt or fruit

INFORMAL SUPPERS

Pistou
Wholewheat rolls
Cheese and fruit

Spaghetti with continental lentil sauce
Lettuce, tomato and green herb salad
Orange water ice

Sliced tomato and onion ring starter
Chick peas with pasta
Green salad
Real ice-cream (made with eggs)

FAMILY MEALS

Melon
Butter bean and leek pie
Mashed potatoes; spring greens
Gooseberry fool

Lentil and egg cutlets
Tomato sauce
Carrots; buttered potatoes
Fruit salad

Grapefruit
Continental lentil and walnut loaf
Brown gravy; roast potatoes; Brussels sprouts; apple sauce
Sponge flan with fruit and cream

SPECIAL MEALS

Chilled green pea soup with mint
Stir-fried mixed vegetables, as many colours and varieties as
    possible
Buttered noodles
Cold orange soufflé

Butter beans with mushrooms and coriander
Vegetable rice – brown rice with tomatoes, onions, courgettes,
    aubergines, etc.
Green salad with herbs
Apricot gâteau

Avocado cream with Melba toast
Chilli red bean pancakes
French beans
Strawberries and cream

Chilled cucumber and yoghurt salad with mint
Musakka'a
Buttered spinach; brown rice
Real orange jelly with cream and toasted almonds

Vichysoisse
Red bean moussaka
Broccoli spears; dûchesse potatoes
Chocolate mousse

The Recipes

Sauces and Stocks

As sauces and stock are called for in quite a number of the recipes, I've gathered these basics together into one section, and I'm also including some, such as tomato sauce and brown gravy, which are useful for serving with the finished pulse dishes. (Basic recipes for mayonnaise and yoghurt are at the beginning of the salads section.) Although I use 100 per cent wholewheat flour for most purposes, I find 81 per cent or ordinary white flour better for thickening sauces.

UNSALTED STOCK

Cooking pulses in stock definitely gives the best flavour, but if the stock is salty the pulses do not cook properly. If you've got some home-made vegetable stock, that is undoubtedly the answer; if not, vegetable stock cubes containing only a little salt are available from health shops, and these I've found excellent. Be sure to get the low-salt ones, though. Another good alternative is to use an unsalted yeast extract made up with boiling water. It is sometimes possible to obtain unsalted yeast extract from chemists and health shops; even if they do not have it available they will probably order it for you. The proportions I use are: 1 teaspoon yeast extract to ¾-1 pint (400-550 ml) hot water.

BASIC WHITE SAUCE

1 oz (25 g) butter	sea salt
1 oz (25 g) plain flour	freshly ground black pepper
¾ pint (400 ml) milk, preferably hot	grated nutmeg

Melt the butter in a medium-sized saucepan, stir in the flour and let it cook for a minute or two, but don't let it brown, then remove from the heat and add the milk. I find that a small balloon whisk is excellent for this and if you also heat the milk, you'll find that it goes in easily every time and you'll always have a nice smooth sauce. When you've added the milk, put the saucepan back over the heat and go on whisking as the sauce thickens, then turn the heat down and let the sauce simmer very gently for 15 minutes to cook the flour and reduce the sauce to the right consistency. Season with sea salt, freshly ground black pepper and nutmeg. You could also flavour the sauce with a bayleaf or a bouquet garni: simmer these in the milk for a minute or two, then leave them in the hot milk for 15 minutes, taking them out before using the milk to make the sauce.

CHEESE SAUCE

Make this as above, adding 4 oz (125 g) grated cheese after removing the sauce from the heat when it has thickened and cooked. You won't need as much salt, because of the cheese, but ¼-½ teaspoon of dry mustard gives cheese sauce a pleasant 'bite'.

PARSLEY SAUCE

Stir 2-3 tablespoons finely chopped parsley into the finished
white sauce.

QUICK BLENDER WHITE SAUCE

This is the method that I use most of the time; it's so labour-
saving and I find the sauce is just as good as that made by the
traditional method. Parsley sauce is particularly easy when
made by this method because you don't have to chop the
parsley, simply pop the sprigs into the blender with everything
else:

1 oz (25 g) butter	sea salt
1 oz (25 g) flour	freshly ground black pepper
¾ pint (400 ml) milk	

Put the butter, flour and milk into the liquidizer goblet;
add about ½ teaspoon of sea salt and a good grinding of
black pepper. Blend at high speed for a few seconds to break
up the butter and mix everything together. There will be some
lumpy bits of butter, but that doesn't matter. Turn the mixture
into a medium-sized saucepan and put over a moderate heat,
stir the sauce until it has thickened, then turn down the heat
and leave the sauce to simmer gently for 15 minutes. The
cooking is particularly important with this sauce because there
has been no initial cooking of the flour, as in traditional
saucemaking, and so you must allow time for this, or the sauce
will have a raw, 'floury' taste.

QUICK BLENDER CHEESE SAUCE

For a quick cheese sauce, add 4 oz (125 g) grated cheese after the sauce has cooked.

QUICK BLENDER PARSLEY SAUCE

Put some sprigs of parsley into the liquidizer with the other ingredients at the beginning of the process.

BASIC TOMATO SAUCE

1 large onion, peeled and chopped
1 large clove garlic, crushed
3 tablespoons vegetable oil
14 oz (397 g) can tomatoes
1-2 tablespoons tomato purée
sea salt
freshly ground black pepper
sugar

Fry the onion and garlic in the oil in a good-sized saucepan until they're soft but not brown – about 10 minutes, then add the tomatoes and tomato purée. Bring the mixture up to the boil and let it simmer away fairly vigorously, without a lid on the saucepan, for 10-15 minutes, to reduce the liquid and bring the sauce to a purée-like consistency. Season carefully with sea salt, freshly ground black pepper and perhaps a little sugar, which I think often makes all the difference to a tomato sauce. You can sieve or liquidize it if you want a smooth texture.

Of course that's just the basic sauce, and there are all sorts of other things you can add to it to make it a bit different. It's lovely with a little red wine added – put this in with the tomato purée – or with some oregano or basil. A bouquet garni or just a bayleaf are also good – you can add these right at the beginning when you're frying the onion – and some chilli powder and/or cinnamon make the sauce more spicy.

APPLE SAUCE

2 medium-sized cooking apples	4 tablespoons sugar
4 tablespoons water	1 oz (25 g) butter
	sea salt

Peel and core the apples, then cut them into smallish pieces. Put the apple pieces, water, sugar and butter into a medium-sized heavy-based saucepan and cook gently, with a lid on the saucepan, until the apples are soft. Season with a little sea salt, and mash the mixture slightly with a wooden spoon, if necessary, to break up the apple. (Or you can sieve or liquidize it if you prefer a smooth consistency.)

BROWN GRAVY

This is really just a quick, simple savoury sauce and it's what I, as a vegetarian, make for gravy. The flavour depends very much on the quality of the stock used – see page 61.

1 onion, peeled and chopped	parsley, a sprig of thyme
2 tablespoons oil	and a bayleaf, tied together
1 rounded tablespoon flour	¾ pint (400 ml) hot stock
1 clove garlic, crushed	sea salt
bouquet garni – a sprig of	freshly ground black pepper

Brown the onion in the oil, then add the flour and continue cooking until that is nutbrown too. Then add the garlic, bouquet garni, and stock, and simmer gently without a lid on the saucepan to cook the flour and reduce the sauce to a good consistency. Strain before serving; season with sea salt and freshly ground black pepper

---

CURRY SAUCE – ENGLISH STYLE

1 onion, peeled and chopped	¾ pint (400 ml) stock *or* water
1 apple, peeled and chopped	1 tablespoon tomato purée
2 tablespoons oil	sea salt
1 tablespoon curry powder	freshly ground black pepper
1 oz (25 g) flour	lemon juice

Fry the onion and apple in the oil in a medium-sized saucepan for 10 minutes, without browning, then add the curry powder and fry for a further 1-2 minutes. Stir in the flour and cook for 2 minutes, then remove the saucepan from the heat and mix in the stock or water and tomato purée. Return the saucepan to the heat and bring up to the boil, stirring all the time. Let the sauce simmer gently for 15 minutes without a lid on the saucepan, then season with sea salt and freshly ground black pepper and a squeeze of lemon juice if you think it's necessary. You can serve this sauce as it is or liquidize it if you prefer it smooth.

CURRY SAUCE – INDIAN STYLE

4 tablespoons oil
1 clove garlic, crushed
1 onion, peeled and chopped
2½ teaspoons ground coriander
2½ teaspoons ground cumin
½ teaspoon curry powder

½ teaspoon turmeric
1 bayleaf
8 oz (225 g) canned tomatoes
¾ pint (400 ml) stock
1 teaspoon garam masala
sea salt
freshly ground black pepper

Heat the oil in a medium-sized saucepan and add the crushed garlic and chopped onion. Fry gently until the onion is soft and lightly browned, about 10 minutes, then add all the spices and the bayleaf, cook for 2 minutes longer. Mix in the tomatoes and stock and simmer gently for 15 minutes, without a lid on the saucepan. Stir in the garam masala and sea salt and freshly ground black pepper to taste. Serve the sauce as it is, or liquidize or sieve it if you prefer.

This sauce is not 'hot', but it's very flavoursome and useful for serving with pulses.

Soups

Making dried peas, beans and lentils into soup is one of the oldest and most basic of all cooking techniques and one which has produced subsistence food for generations the world over. Almost every country seems to have its pea, bean or lentil soup, from the spicy dal soups of India and the fasolada of Greece to the chick pea and garlic soup of Spain and the bean soup of the USA, which, incidentally, appears on the menu in the restaurant of the House of Representatives every day. Legend has it that one hot summer's day in 1904 the Speaker, Joseph G. (Uncle Joe) Cannon, ordered bean soup and was told it was unavailable. He caused a great furore, saying that from then on it must appear on the menu daily, come rain or shine, snow-storm or tropical heatwave, and the US Embassy confirms that this indeed happen.

It is not difficult to make soup from pulses; in fact I think it's easier than making fresh vegetable soups, because the pulses need so little preparation. With the exception of the quick-cooking split red lentils, I do think it is worth trying to make time to soak the pulses, though, because not only does this speed up the cooking time, it also makes them more digestible, as I've explained on page 37.

Although they can be very filling – and some of these soups, such as the pistou and the thick butter bean and tomato soup, are real rib-stickers and make a meal in themselves – pulse soups don't have to be so substantial, because it's easy to vary their character by the amount of liquid you use and how you present them. For instance, it would be hard to get two soups more different than the filling pistou soup from the South of France, which you can just about stand a spoon up in, and the

thin, elegant haricot bean and watercress soup yet they both
have haricot beans as their basis.

BEAN AND CARROT SOUP

The recipe for this soup is based on a wartime one. The result
is a pretty, pale golden soup with a creamy consistency, and
the combination of beans and milk is excellent from the protein
point of view.

4 oz (125 g) haricot beans,
  soaked, drained and rinsed
1½ pints (850 ml) unsalted
  stock *or* water
1 large onion, peeled and
  sliced
1 stick of celery, sliced
2 large carrots, scraped and
  diced
a bouquet garni – a sprig or
  two of parsley, a sprig of

thyme and a bayleaf, tied
  together
1 oz (25 g) butter
1 oz (25 g) flour
½ pint (275 ml) milk
sea salt
freshly ground black pepper
grated nutmeg

To serve:
a little chopped parsley

SERVES 4-5

Put the beans into a large saucepan with the stock or water and
simmer them gently for 45 minutes, then add the onion, celery,
carrots and the bouquet garni and cook them all for another 30
minutes or so until the beans and vegetables are tender. Remove
the bouquet garni and sieve or liquidize the soup.

Melt the butter in a large, clean saucepan and stir in the
flour; when it 'froths', remove the saucepan from the heat
and stir in the puréed soup. Put the saucepan back on the heat

and stir the soup until it has thickened; leave it to simmer gently for 10-15 minutes to cook the flour, then mix in the milk and season the soup with sea salt, freshly ground black pepper and some grated nutmeg. Reheat the soup, but don't let it boil. Serve it sprinkled with chopped parsley.

BUTTER BEAN AND TOMATO SOUP

Served with garlic bread and a salad or some fruit, this hearty soup makes a complete meal.

8 oz (225 g) butter beans
1½ pints (850 ml) water *or* unsalted stock
1 bayleaf
2 large onions
1 oz (25 g) butter
1 lb (450 g) tomatoes, peeled and chopped (or use canned ones)
sea salt
freshly ground black pepper
a little sugar

To serve:
chopped parsley

SERVES 3-4

Soak the butter beans in cold water for several hours, then drain and rinse them as usual. Put them into a large saucepan with the water or stock and the bayleaf and simmer them until tender – about 1¼ hours. Meanwhile, peel and slice the onions and fry them lightly in the butter until they're soft, about 10 minutes, then add them to the cooked butter beans, together with the tomatoes and some sea salt and freshly ground black pepper. Bring them up to the boil and simmer gently for about 10 minutes. Check seasoning, adding more sea salt and freshly ground black pepper and a little sugar if you think it needs them. Serve sprinkled with the parsley. You can liquidize this soup, if you prefer – remove the bayleaf first!

CHILLED SPLIT GREEN PEA SOUP WITH MINT

If you normally think of pulse soups as filling, cold-weather food, do try this soup which comes from the USA and is served chilled. It makes a useful protein-rich starter for the summer and is very refreshing.

2 tablespoons vegetable oil
1 large onion, peeled and chopped
1 stick of celery, chopped
8 sprigs of fresh mint
4 oz (125 g) split green peas, washed
1¾ pints (1 l) unsalted stock

pinch of ground cloves
1 bayleaf
sea salt
freshly ground black pepper

To serve:
a little single cream

SERVES 4

Heat the oil in a large saucepan, add the onion and celery and fry them gently, without browning, for about 10 minutes. Meanwhile remove the leaves from the stems of the mint; chop the leaves and put them on one side. Tie the stalks together and put them into the saucepan with the onion and celery, together with the split peas, the stock, ground cloves and bayleaf. Half-cover the saucepan with a lid and let it simmer gently for about 40 minutes, until the split peas are tender. Remove the bayleaf and mint stalks and liqui ize the soup; season it carefully to taste. Put the soup into a bowl and leave it to cool, then chill it. Taste the soup before serving (chilling tends to dull the flavour of food). Spoon the soup into individual bowls and top each portion with a swirl of cream and the reserved chopped mint leaves.

CONTINENTAL LENTIL AND MUSHROOM SOUP

The lentils and mushrooms in this soup blend beautifully in flavour and texture – if they don't know, people may think they're just eating mushroom soup, but of course the lentils make it full of nourishment.

4 oz (125 g) continental lentils
1 large onion
1 large clove garlic
1 oz (25 g) butter
4 oz (125 g) mushrooms
1½ pints (850 ml) water *or* un-

salted stock
sea salt
freshly ground black pepper

To serve:
2 tablespoons chopped parsley

SERVES 4-5

Wash, soak, drain and rinse the continental lentils as usual. Peel and chop the onion and crush the garlic, then fry them together in the butter in a large saucepan for 5 minutes. Wash and chop the mushrooms and add them to the onions and garlic in the saucepan; fry for a further 4-5 minutes, then add the rinsed and drained lentils and the water or stock. Simmer gently, with a lid on the saucepan, for about an hour, until the lentils are tender. Then liquidize the soup and season it with sea salt and freshly ground black pepper. Return the soup to the rinsed-out saucepan to reheat it, and serve it sprinkled with the parsley.

CONTINENTAL LENTIL AND VEGETABLE SOUP

You can liquidize this soup if you want to, but personally I prefer not to; it looks attractive with the whole brown lentils and the colourful pieces of vegetable.

4 oz (125 g) continental lentils
1 oz (25 g) butter
1 onion, peeled and chopped
1 large clove garlic, crushed
2 large carrots, scraped and cut into small dice
2 sticks celery, thinly sliced
2 tomatoes, skinned and chopped
2 oz (50 g) mushrooms, wiped and chopped
3-4 oz (75-100 g) cabbage, washed and chopped
1¾ pints (1 l) unsalted stock
a bouquet garni – a couple of sprigs of parsley, a sprig of thyme and a bayleaf, tied together
2 tablespoons chopped parsley
sea salt
freshly ground black pepper

SERVES 4-5

Soak the lentils in water for several hours, then drain and rinse them. Melt the butter in a large saucepan and fry the onion for 5 minutes, but don't brown it, then add the garlic and all the other vegetables and cook them very gently for a further 5 minutes, stirring often to prevent sticking. Mix in the drained lentils and stir for a minute or two so that the lentils get coated with the butter, then put in the stock and the bouquet garni.

Bring the mixture up to the boil, then cover it and leave it to simmer for about 1¼ hours, or until the lentils are tender. Remove the bunch of herbs; stir in the chopped parsley and some sea salt and freshly ground black pepper to taste. This soup is nice served with grated cheese and some warm, crusty rolls.

CREAM OF BUTTER BEAN SOUP

As this soup has a smooth, creamy texture, I like to serve it with some crunchy croûtons of fried bread scattered over the top.

4 oz (125 g) butter beans
1 large onion
1 medium-sized potato
2 carrots
2 sticks celery
1 oz (25 g) butter
1½ pints (850 ml) water *or* unsalted stock
½ pint (275 ml) milk
a bouquet garni – a couple of

sprigs of parsley, a sprig of thyme and a bayleaf, tied together
4-6 tablespoons cream
sea salt
freshly ground black pepper
grated nutmeg

To serve:
a few croûtons of fried bread

SERVES 4-6

Soak the butter beans, then drain and rinse them. Peel and chop the onion and potato; scrape and chop the carrots; slice the celery. Melt the butter in a large saucepan and add the vegetables; sauté them for 7-8 minutes, but don't let them brown, then add the butter beans, water or stock, the milk and the bouquet garni. Simmer gently, with a lid half on the saucepan, for about 1¼ hours, or until the butter beans are tender. Remove the herbs, then liquidize the soup, stir in the cream and add sea salt, freshly ground black pepper and nutmeg to taste. Reheat the soup, but don't let it boil. Serve each bowl sprinkled with croûtons.

CREAM OF HARICOT BEAN SOUP

8 oz (225 g) haricot beans
1¾ pints (1 l) unsalted stock
a bouquet garni – sprig each of parsley and thyme and a bayleaf
1 onion, peeled and chopped
2 cloves garlic, crushed

1 oz (25 g) butter
¼ pint (150 ml) single cream
sea salt
freshly ground black pepper

To serve:
2 tablespoons chopped parsley

SERVES 4-6

Soak, drain and rinse the beans as usual, then put them into a large saucepan with the stock and the bouquet garni. Bring them up to the boil, then simmer them gently, with a lid on the saucepan, for about 1 hour, until the beans are tender. Remove the bouquet garni and liquidize the soup or pass it through a vegetable mill. Return the soup to a clean saucepan.

Fry the onion and garlic in the butter in a small saucepan for about 10 minutes, until the onion is tender but not browned. Stir this onion mixture into the soup, together with the cream and some sea salt and freshly ground black pepper to taste. Reheat the soup, but do not let it boil. Serve it sprinkled with the chopped parsley.

DAL SOUP

One of my favourite soups, this is ideal for serving before a rice and curry meal because the pulse protein complements the rice, giving first-class nourishment. You can use either split peas or split red lentils.

6 oz (175 g) yellow split peas *or* split red lentils	1 teaspoon ground ginger
	1 bayleaf
1 large onion	1¾ pints (1 l) water
2 tablespoons oil	1 lemon
1 clove garlic, crushed	sea salt
1 teaspoon turmeric	freshly ground black pepper

SERVES 4-5

Cover the split peas or split red lentils with water and leave them to soak for a few hours; drain and rinse them. Peel and chop the onion and fry it in the oil in a large saucepan for 5 minutes, then add the garlic, turmeric, ginger and bayleaf and fry for a further 5 minutes. Stir in the split peas or lentils and the water. Bring the mixture up to the boil, then let it simmer gently, with a lid on the saucepan, for about 30 minutes, or until the lentils or split peas are soft. Remove the bayleaf and liquidize the soup. Wash the lemon, then cut four or five nice circles from it, one to garnish each bowl of soup. Squeeze the rest of the lemon and add enough of the juice to the soup to sharpen it; season carefully with sea salt and freshly ground black pepper. Reheat the soup and serve each bowlful with a circle of lemon floating in it.

DRIED WHOLE PEA SOUP

4 oz (125 g) dried whole peas
4 cloves
1 large onion, peeled but not chopped
2 good sprigs of mint
1½ pints (850 ml) water *or* unsalted stock
2 teaspoons sugar

1 teaspoon lemon juice
sea salt
freshly ground black pepper
1 oz (25 g) butter

To serve:
chopped fresh mint leaves

SERVES 4

Soak the peas for several hours in plenty of cold water, then drain and rinse them. Stick the cloves into the onion and put it into a large saucepan, together with the peas, mint and water or stock. Simmer gently for about 1 hour, until the peas are very tender. Remove the cloves from the onion, then liquidize the soup, with the onion and sprigs of mint, until it's really smooth. Stir in the sugar and lemon juice and season with plenty of sea salt and freshly ground black pepper. Return the soup to the rinsed-out saucepan to reheat it; add the butter just before serving. Garnish each bowl of soup with some chopped fresh mint leaves.

FASOLADA

The most popular way of eating dried beans in Greece is in the form of this soup, sometimes called 'the national dish of

Greece', although also considered to be rather basic, subsistence food, like our pease pudding and baked beans. It's a tasty, warming soup if well made; I do think the olive oil is essential to give the right flavour.

6 tablespoons olive oil

1 large onion, peeled and chopped

2 sticks celery, sliced

2 carrots, scraped and chopped

1 clove garlic, crushed

8 oz (225 g) haricot beans, soaked, thoroughly rinsed

and then drained

1¾ pints (1 l) unsalted stock *or* water

1 tablespoon tomato purée

2 tablespoons chopped parsley

sea salt

freshly ground black pepper

a little lemon juice

SERVES 4

Heat the oil in a large saucepan and fry the onion, celery, carrot and garlic for 5 minutes, stirring them from time to time to prevent sticking. Then stir in the drained beans, stock or water, tomato purée and parsley and bring the mixture up to the boil. Cover the saucepan with a lid, reduce heat and simmer soup gently for about 1 hour, until the beans are tender. Season with sea salt and freshly ground black pepper to taste and a little lemon juice if you think it needs it.

This soup can be served as it is, or liquidized; personally I think it's nicest when it's been liquidized. Wholewheat rolls go well with it and of course the wheat complements the bean protein to give good nourishment.

FLAGEOLET SOUP

Creamy and delicate, this soup is equally nice served hot or cold. If serving it cold, use oil, not butter, chill the soup well, and garnish it with extra cream and some chopped chives. The green leek helps to accentuate the natural green colour of the beans.

4 oz (125 g) flageolet beans
1 small onion
1 leek
1 oz (25 g) butter
1½ pints (850 ml) unsalted stock *or* water
2-4 tablespoons double cream

1 tablespoon chopped parsley
sea salt
freshly ground black pepper

To serve:
a little chopped fresh parsley

SERVES 4

Soak, rinse and drain the beans as usual. Peel and chop the onion; thoroughly wash and shred the leek, including as much of the green part as possible, then cook them gently together in the butter in a good-sized saucepan for about 10 minutes. Add the beans to the onion and leek, together with the stock or water, and simmer gently for about 1 hour, until the beans are tender. Put the soup into the liquidizer goblet with the cream and parsley and blend to a smooth, creamy consistency. Season with sea salt and freshly ground black pepper. Reheat but do not boil soup; serve garnished with extra chopped parsley.

HARICOT BEAN AND
WATERCRESS SOUP

The flavour of the watercress comes through strongly in this soup, while the beans supply protein.

6 oz (175 g) haricot beans
1 bunch watercress
1 oz (25 g) butter
1 onion, peeled and chopped

1¾ pints (1 l) water *or* un-
    salted stock
sea salt
freshly ground black pepper

SERVES 4-6

Soak the beans as usual, then drain and rinse them. Wash the watercress, separating the leaves from the coarse stems; chop the stems. Melt the butter in a large saucepan, add the onion and fry it gently for 5 minutes, without browning, then add the chopped watercress stalks and fry for a further few minutes. Mix in the beans and water or stock and bring up to the boil; simmer for about 1 hour, until the beans are tender. Put the soup and the reserved watercress leaves into the liquidizer goblet and blend until smooth (do this in two batches if necessary). Return the soup to the rinsed-out saucepan, adjusting the consistency with a little extra stock if necessary. Season with sea salt and freshly ground black pepper.

LENTIL SOUP WITH
CURRIED CROÛTONS

You can vary the thickness of this soup very easily according to the quantity of lentils you use. The amount I've given is right for a rather thin soup (my preference), but for something thicker and more substantial use 6-8 oz (175-225 g) lentils.

1 oz (25 g) butter
1 onion, peeled and chopped
1 carrot, scraped and sliced
4 oz (125 g) lentils
1½ pints (850 ml) unsalted stock
1 bayleaf
½ pint (275 ml) milk

2 teaspoons lemon juice
sea salt
freshly ground black pepper

For the croûtons:
3 slices of bread
oil for shallow frying
1 teaspoon curry powder

SERVES 6

Melt the butter in a large saucepan; add the onion and carrot and fry them together until they're lightly browned. Wash and drain the lentils and mix them in with the onion and carrot; stir for a minute or two so that all the lentils get coated with the butter, then pour in the stock and add the bayleaf. Bring up to the boil, then turn down the heat and let the mixture simmer gently for about 30 minutes, until the lentils and vegetables are cooked.

While the soup is cooking, make the croûtons. Remove the crusts from the slices of bread, then cut the bread into ¼ inch (6 mm) dice. Heat a little oil in a frying pan and add the bread; sprinkle in the curry powder. Turn the pieces of bread in the oil so that they get crisp all over and the curry powder is well distributed. Drain the croûtons on kitchen paper.

Sieve or liquidize the soup. Add enough milk to bring it to a creamy consistency, then mix in the lemon juice and plenty of sea salt and freshly ground black pepper to taste. Reheat the soup gently, but don't let it boil. Serve the soup in individual bowls with a few of the croûtons on top of each portion.

LENTIL SOUP WITH GARLIC AND CUMIN

Here's a recipe for lentil soup as it's often served in Egypt, where it's known as 'shurit ads'. I like the spicy flavour of this soup very much.

8 oz (225 g) split red lentils	2 large cloves garlic, crushed
2 pints (1.3 l) unsalted stock	1 oz (25 g) butter
1 large onion, peeled and chopped	1-2 teaspoons ground cumin sea salt
1 tomato, peeled and sliced	freshly ground black pepper

SERVES 4-6

Wash and pick over the lentils, then put them into a large saucepan with the stock, half the onion, the tomato and the garlic. Bring up to the boil, then simmer gently for about half an hour, until the lentils are cooked.

Meanwhile, melt half the butter in a small saucepan and fry the remaining onion until it's soft and golden.

Liquidize the soup and add the remaining butter, the cumin and sea salt and freshly ground black pepper to taste. Serve the soup with the fried onion floating on top as a garnish.

LENTIL AND TOMATO SOUP

Although it's generally best to avoid cooking pulses with tomatoes because the acid can prevent them from softening properly, in this recipe the presence of a good quantity of stock, and the fact that split red lentils are quick-cooking, means that one can get away with it and the result is a lovely tasty soup.

1 large onion	stock *or* water
1 stick of celery	sea salt
2 tablespoons oil	freshly ground black pepper
4 oz (125 g) split red lentils, washed	1-2 tablespoons lemon juice
14 oz (397 g) can tomatoes	*To serve:*
1½ pints (850 ml) unsalted	a little chopped parsley

SERVES 4

Peel and finely chop the onion; slice the celery. Heat the oil in a large saucepan and fry the onion and celery for 7-10 minutes without browning them, then stir in the lentils and mix for a minute or two so that the lentils get coated with the oil. Add the tomatoes and stock or water to the saucepan and bring up to the boil. Half-cover with a lid and simmer gently for 25-30 minutes, by which time the lentils should be cooked. Liquidize the soup then return it to the rinsed-out saucepan and season it with sea salt, freshly ground black pepper and lemon juice to taste. Reheat the soup, then serve it garnished with chopped parsley, fresh green against the orange.

PISTOU

Pistou soup came originally from Italy where it was named after the *pesto* or sauce of pounded basil, oil, pine nuts and cheese with which it was flavoured. When the soup crossed the border into France, 'pesto' became 'pistou', and now pistou is generally associated with the South of France, where it is widely made. You really want to use fresh basil for this soup if you possibly can, though fresh parsley mixed with dried basil makes a passable substitute.

8 oz (225 g) haricot beans
2 onions, peeled and chopped
3 tablespoons oil
2 carrots, scraped and diced
2 potatoes, peeled and cut into chunks
8 oz (225 g) courgettes, washed and sliced
4 oz (125 g) French beans, cut into 1 inch (2.5 cm) pieces
1 lb (450 g) tomatoes, skinned and chopped (you can use canned ones)
3 pints (1.7 l) unsalted stock

or water
sea salt
freshly ground black pepper
a little sugar
2 oz (50 g) vermicelli

For the pistou flavouring:
5 cloves garlic
bunch of fresh basil
5 tablespoons olive oil (I often use half vegetable, half olive)
2 tablespoons tomato purée

SERVES 6

Soak the beans as usual, then drain and rinse them. Put them into a saucepan, cover with water, and cook gently until they're just tender. Drain them, reserving their cooking liquor.

Fry the onion in the oil in a large saucepan for 5-10 minutes, then add all the other vegetables and cook for another 4-5 minutes, stirring often to prevent sticking. Mix in the haricot beans, together with their cooking liquid, made up to 3 pints (1.7 l) with extra water or stock. Bring the mixture up to the boil, then let it simmer until the vegetables are nearly tender. Put in the vermicelli and cook for about 10 more minutes, until it's done and all the vegetables are fully cooked. Season with sea salt, freshly ground black pepper and perhaps a dash of sugar.

While all this is going on, you can make the pistou. Crush the garlic and basil to a smooth green paste and stir in the oil and tomato purée. (Use a pestle and mortar for this, or, having crushed the garlic, put everything in the liquidizer and blend until smooth.)

Mix the pistou into the soup just before serving; check seasoning. It's lovely with lots of grated cheese and hunks of crusty bread.

RED SOUP

People react differently to this wartime soup; I love the rich, ruby colour, but my husband finds it off-putting. But it's cheap and a bit different and certainly worth trying, especially if you can serve each bowlful in a most un-wartime way, with a swirl of single cream.

1 onion	1¾ pints (1 l) water *or* un-
1 cooked beetroot	salted vegetable stock
1 tomato	sea salt
1 stick celery	freshly ground black pepper
2 tablespoons vegetable oil	1 tablespoon lemon juice
4 oz (125 g) split red lentils	

SERVES 6

Peel and chop the onion, beetroot and tomato; wash and slice the celery. Heat the oil in a large saucepan and fry all the prepared vegetables gently for about 5 minutes, stirring from time to time. Wash the lentils and add them to the vegetables, along with the water or stock. Bring up to the boil, then simmer the soup gently for about 30 minutes, or until everything is cooked. Liquidize the soup, then season it carefully with sea salt, freshly ground black pepper and lemon juice. Return the soup to the rinsed-out saucepan and reheat it before serving.

SIMPLE LENTIL SOUP

This is my favourite emergency soup. I make it when I find I've suddenly got to produce food for lots of people in the minimum of time. It takes 10-15 minutes with the aid of a pressure cooker, or about 30 minutes without. The butter and garlic are essential to the flavour, but apart from them you can really flavour it up as you like.

1 large onion	water
1 oz (25 g) butter	1 tablespoon lemon juice
1 large clove garlic, crushed	sea salt
4 oz (125 g) split red lentils	freshly ground black pepper
1½ pints (850 ml) stock *or*	

SERVES 4-5

Peel and chop the onion, then fry it in the butter in a large

86

saucepan or pressure cooker pan for 5 minutes; add the garlic and lentils and stir for a minute, then pour in the stock or water. Bring up to the boil and simmer for 15 minutes or so or pressure cook at 15 lbs for 5 minutes, until lentils are cooked. Liquidize, then add the lemon juice and sea salt and freshly ground black pepper to taste. You can make it thicker, if you prefer, by using 2-4 oz (50-100 g) more lentils.

SPANISH CHICK PEA SOUP
WITH GARLIC AND MINT

Chick peas are used a lot in Spanish cookery, and in this soup, 'sopa de panela', their flavour combines beautifully with the mint and garlic.

8 oz (225 g) chick peas
2 cloves garlic, crushed
a handful of mint, stalks removed
a small handful of parsley, stalks removed

6 tablespoons olive oil
sea salt
freshly ground black pepper
2 slices of bread, crusts removed

SERVES 4

Soak the chick peas for several hours, then drain and rinse them. Put the chick peas into a saucepan and cover them generously with water; simmer until they're very tender, then drain them and measure the liquid. Put the chick peas, 1½ pints (850 ml) of their liquid (made up with extra water if necessary), the garlic, mint, parsley and half the oil into the liquidizer goblet (it may be necessary to do this in two batches) and blend at high speed until smooth. Season with sea salt and freshly ground black pepper and reheat gently. While this is happening, cut the bread into little cubes and fry it in the remaining oil until golden brown. Serve the soup sprinkled with the fried bread croûtons.

SPINACH AND LENTIL SOUP

Richly flavoured and satisfying, this is a lovely warming soup to serve on a cold day.

4 oz (125 g) continental lentils
1 large onion
1 oz (25 g) butter
1 large clove garlic, crushed
1¾ pints (1 l) unsalted stock *or* water
8 oz (225 g) spinach

sea salt
freshly ground black pepper
2-3 teaspoons lemon juice

To serve:
croûtons *or* a little single cream

SERVES 4

Wash the lentils and pick them over carefully, then put them into a bowl, cover them with cold water and leave to soak for several hours. Then drain and rinse them. Peel and chop the onion and fry it in the butter in a large saucepan for 10 minutes, until it's soft but not browned. Add the rinsed and drained lentils and the garlic and stir them for a minute or two so that they all get coated with the butter, then pour in the stock or water. Bring the mixture up to the boil, then let it simmer gently for about 45 minutes, until the lentils are soft. (You can of course use a pressure cooker for this, and in fact I usually do. In this case, fry the onion in the pressure cooker pan and proceed as above, cooking the soup under pressure for about 15 minutes.)

While the lentils are cooking, wash the spinach in several changes of cold water, then chop it roughly. Add the spinach to the cooked lentil mixture, cover and simmer gently for about 10 minutes, until the spinach is soft. Liquidize the soup, then return it to the rinsed-out saucepan and season it with sea salt, freshly ground black pepper and plenty of lemon juice. This soup is very nice as it is, but it's even better if you serve it topped with some crispy fried bread croûtons or a swirl of single cream.

Starters, Salads, Pâtés and Spreads

I know that most people think of beans and lentils in terms of hot, often filling dishes but, perhaps surprisingly, I think they are possibly at their best when served cold as a starter or part of a salad. Few dishes are more delicious, in my opinion, than a smooth, well-made chick pea hummus, all creamy beige, garnished with pale green olive oil, yellow lemon wedges and a flush of red paprika; and, on a hot summer's day, chilled haricot bean salad, glistening with vinaigrette and fragrant with fresh green herbs, is always a treat. And if you're trying to economize, these bean and lentil salads and starters are useful because they provide good protein cheaply, and the rest of the meal can contain that much less – a colourful rice and vegetable mixture, for instance, or vegetables in a light, cheesy sauce.

The important thing to remember when serving pulses chilled is that they must be really well cooked. Not soggy, but certainly very tender, because chilling them firms them up and if they're a little on the under-done side it can make them seem a bit hard. Also, as chilling food tends to dull the flavour, make sure that the mixture is well seasoned. For this reason, it's well worth using a really good quality olive oil when possible and lovely fresh green herbs in the summer.

Although I find a simple vinaigrette dressing – usually 1 part wine vinegar to three parts oil – the most useful for pulses, there are occasions for using both mayonnaise and also natural yoghurt, as in the very delicious aïgroissade from Provence, for instance, and a dollop of mayonnaise or yoghurt is also good with sliced cold lentil loaf, so I'm starting this section with quick recipes for both, so that they're handy if they're needed.

BLENDER MAYONNAISE

Traditional mayonnaise is not really difficult to make, but it is time-consuming, so I generally use this quick blender method which makes excellent mayonnaise in a fraction of the time.

1 whole egg
¼ teaspoon sea salt
¼ teaspoon dry mustard
¼ teaspoon freshly ground black pepper

2 teaspoons wine vinegar
2 teaspoons lemon juice
7 fl. oz. (200 ml) salad oil
1-2 tablespoons boiling water

MAKES 7 FL. OZ. (200 ml)

Put the whole egg, sea salt, mustard, freshly ground black pepper, vinegar and lemon juice into the liquidizer goblet and blend at medium speed for about 1 minute. Then turn the speed to high and gradually add the oil, drop by drop, through the hole in the lid of the liquidizer goblet. When about half of the oil has been added, you will hear the sound change to a 'glug-glug' noise, and then you can add the remaining oil more quickly, in a thin stream. Finally, stir in the boiling water to thin the mixture to the required consistency. This mayonnaise keeps very well for up to a fortnight in the refrigerator.

YOGHURT

Yoghurt should be smooth and creamy and firm enough to cut with a spoon. It's very easy to make at home and you don't need any fancy equipment.

1 pint (575 ml) silver top milk
2 rounded tablespoons skim milk powder
1 teaspoon fresh natural yoghurt (*or* a teaspoonful saved from the previous batch)

Put the milk into a saucepan and bring it up to the boil, then let it simmer for 10 minutes. It's helpful to have one of those glass 'milk savers' in the saucepan for this to prevent the milk from boiling over. (This boiling process reduces the milk a little and so helps to make the yoghurt nice and thick and creamy.) Then take the saucepan off the heat and leave it until the milk has cooled to lukewarm. Remove the 'milk saver' if you've used one, and beat the skim milk powder and yoghurt into the milk (I often use a liquidizer to do this). Then pour the milk into a clean, sterilized bowl or a couple of sterilized jars, cover with foil, and leave in a warm place until firm.

To sterilize the bowl or jars (and the liquidizer goblet, if I'm using that too), I swish them out with some hot water to which I've added a teaspoonful of household bleach, then rinse them; and for the 'warm place' I use the airing cupboard or stand the yoghurt near the pilot light on my gas cooker.

Once the yoghurt has 'set', it should be put into the refrigerator, where it will firm up even more, and is then ready for use when required.

AÏGROISSADE

Strictly speaking this Provençal salad consists of tender young vegetables and chick peas, cooked and cooled and mixed with aioli, that special garlic dressing which is like mayonnaise. I tend to cheat a bit by simply adding crushed garlic to some of my own blender mayonnaise, and I generally use a mixture of half mayonnaise and half natural yoghurt, as in this recipe, as it's lighter and less fattening. Anyway, the result always seems to go down very well, so much so that I find I'm making it all the year round, using the vegetables available, not just in the summer!

8 oz (225 g) new potatoes
4 oz (125 g) new carrots
4 oz (125 g) shelled broad beans
4 oz (125 g) French beans
14 oz (397 g) can artichoke hearts
4 oz (125 g) chick peas, soaked, drained and rinsed, then cooked until tender and drained

1 large clove garlic, crushed, or more, according to taste
6 rounded tablespoons mayonnaise
6 rounded tablespoons natural yoghurt
sea salt
freshly ground black pepper

To serve:
chopped parsley

SERVES 3-4

Scrape the potatoes and carrots and cook them in boiling, salted water until they're nearly tender. Wash the shelled broad beans, top and tail the French beans, and add them to the pan of potatoes and carrots. When all the vegetables are tender, drain and cool them, then cut them into even-sized pieces. Drain and slice the artichoke hearts and mix them with the other vegetables, together with the chick peas. Mix together the garlic, mayonnaise and natural yoghurt, then add the vegetables, turning them gently so that they are all coated with the creamy mayonnaise mixture. Serve sprinkled with chopped parsley. This is very nice with warm wholewheat rolls.

BEAN CURD, CARROT AND SULTANA SALAD

The bean curd in this salad gives excellent protein, so it's really a main course salad. It's good with wholewheat bread and butter and a bowl of crisp lettuce or watercress.

6 oz (175 g) bean curd (see page 53)
2 large carrots
4 oz (125 g) sultanas
2 tablespoons orange juice
1 tablespoon oil
½ teaspoon sugar
¼ teaspoon dry mustard

1 teaspoon soy sauce
sea salt
freshly ground black pepper

To serve:
1 tablespoon chopped chives
   or spring onion greens

SERVES 3

Cut the bean curd into small squares; scrape and coarsely grate the carrots. Wash the sultanas, put them into a small bowl and cover them with boiling water; leave them for 10-15 minutes to plump up, then drain them. Put the bean curd, grated carrot and sultanas into a bowl. In a small bowl beat together the orange juice, oil, sugar, mustard, soy sauce and some sea salt and freshly ground black pepper to taste. Pour this dressing over the carrot mixture and turn salad gently with a spoon

until everything is coated with the dressing, but be careful not
to break up the bean curd. Serve sprinkled with chopped chives
or spring onion greens.

BEAN SPROUT AND CABBAGE SALAD

Cabbage is so useful for salads, particularly in the winter, but
it can be a little dull without other, more exciting ingredients.
In this salad bean sprouts add interest, and the pineapple gives
a pleasant touch of sweetness.

12 oz (350 g) hard white
cabbage
8 oz (225 g) fresh bean
sprouts
14 oz (397 g) can pineapple

chunks, drained
1 tablespoon salad oil
sea salt
freshly ground black pepper
lemon juice

SERVES 4

Wash and finely shred the cabbage and put it into a large bowl.
Wash and drain the bean sprouts; lightly crush the pineapple
with a fork, to break it up a bit. Add the bean sprouts and pineapple to the cabbage, together with the oil, sea salt and freshly
ground black pepper and a little lemon juice to taste. Mix
well.

You might feel you want to add more oil than I have
suggested. Recently I have cut down rather on the amount of
oil I add to salads like this, mainly out of consideration for
people's figures and I find that if the salad contains moist,
juicy ingredients, as in this case, the result is really just as good.

BEAN SPROUT, MUSHROOM
AND CELERY SALAD

A useful salad for winter when the usual salad vegetables are in short supply. If you want to give the salad an unusual, Oriental look, in keeping with the bean sprouts, you can slice the celery diagonally across.

1 large head celery	½ teaspoon dry mustard
8 oz (225 g) bean sprouts	½ teaspoon sugar
6 oz (175 g) very fresh white button mushrooms	1 tablespoon wine vinegar
	sea salt
3 tablespoons oil	freshly ground black pepper
1 teaspoon soy sauce	

SERVES 4

Wash the celery, discarding tough, outer stems; slice the tender stems and put them into a bowl. Rinse the bean sprouts and add them to the celery. Wash the mushrooms gently but thoroughly, then slice them and put them in the bowl with the other vegetables. Make a dressing by mixing together the oil, soy sauce, mustard, sugar, wine vinegar and some sea salt and freshly ground black pepper. Pour the dressing over the vegetables and turn them gently so that they all get coated with it.

BEAN SPROUT, TOMATO AND
ONION SALAD

Whether or not you skin the tomatoes for this salad is very much a matter of choice. Personally I think if the tomatoes are sound and firm it is a shame to skin them, but on the other hand I have a friend who can't stand tomato skins under any circumstances! If you do skin them, be careful not to leave the tomatoes in the boiling water for a second longer than necessary: 1 minute should be ample, then plunge them straight into cold water to prevent further 'cooking'.

12 oz (350 g) bean sprouts
8 oz (225 g) tomatoes
1 mild onion
1 tablespoon oil
1 teaspoon lemon juice
1 tablespoon chopped parsley
sea salt
freshly ground black pepper

SERVES 4

Rinse the bean sprouts; dice the tomatoes; peel and thinly slice the onion, and then put them all into a bowl. Add the oil, lemon juice, parsley and some sea salt and freshly ground black pepper to taste and mix gently but thoroughly.

BEANY SALAD BOWL

6 tablespoons olive oil
2 tablespoons wine vinegar
½ teaspoon dry mustard
1 teaspoon sugar
sea salt
freshly ground black pepper
4 oz (125 g) beans – any type, chick peas, butter beans, or some of the more unusual ones, soaked and cooked until tender, then drained

2 tablespoons chopped fresh green herbs
1 heart of celery
1 green pepper, de-seeded and sliced
2 large carrots, scraped and coarsely grated
4 inch (10 cm) cucumber, diced
1 apple, diced

SERVES 4

Into a salad bowl put the oil, vinegar, mustard, sugar, some sea salt and a good grinding of black pepper. Give it a good stir, so that it's all blended, then add the beans, green herbs and the rest of the ingredients and mix well so that everything gets coated with the dressing. It's nice served with home-made wholewheat bread and unsalted butter, and of course the wheat protein complements the bean protein to give excellent nourishment.

BUTTER BEAN, APPLE AND BEETROOT SALAD

4 oz (125 g) butter bean
1 teaspoon honey
3 tablespoons oil
1 tablespoon red wine vinegar
sea salt
freshly ground black pepper

1 large, cooked beetroot
2 sweet eating apples

To serve:
a little chopped fresh mint

SERVES 2-3

Soak and then cook the butter beans as usual; drain them well. Make a dressing by mixing together the honey, oil, vinegar and some sea salt and freshly ground black pepper and pour this over the butter beans, turning them gently in it. Peel and dice the beetroot; wash, core and slice the apples, and add them to the beans. Mix gently, then chill the salad and serve it garnished with chopped mint.

BUTTER BEANS AND MUSH-ROOMS WITH CORIANDER

This is one of my favourite bean salads, succulent and spicy. It makes an excellent starter. Serve it with soft rolls to mop up the delicious juices.

4 oz (125 g) butter beans
8 oz (225 g) small white button mushrooms
8 tablespoons vegetable oil
3-4 teaspoons ground coriander
2 cloves garlic, crushed

juice of 1 lemon
sea salt
freshly ground black pepper

To serve:
crisp lettuce leaves
chopped parsley

SERVES 4 AS A STARTER,
2 AS A MAIN SALAD DISH

Soak the butter beans for several hours in cold water, then drain and rinse them, cover them with fresh water, simmer them gently until they're tender, then drain them. Wash the mushrooms and halve or quarter them if necessary. Heat the oil in a saucepan and add the mushrooms and coriander. Fry the mushrooms for 1-2 minutes, just to tenderize them, but don't let them get soggy. Remove the pan from the heat and add the butter beans, garlic and lemon juice. Mix gently, adding sea salt and freshly ground black pepper to taste. Let the mixture cool, then chill it, and serve it on a base of crisp lettuce, garnished with chopped parsley.

BUTTER BEAN, TOMATO AND ONION SALAD

1 clove garlic, crushed
3 tablespoons oil
1 tablespoon wine vinegar
sea salt
freshly ground black pepper
4 oz (125 g) butter beans,
soaked, cooked and drained
1 onion, peeled and sliced into rings
3 firm tomatoes, sliced
a few black olives, if available

SERVES 2-3

Put the garlic, oil, vinegar and some sea salt and freshly ground black pepper into a bowl and mix them well together, then stir in the butter beans, being careful not to mash them, and the onion, tomatoes and olives. Turn them gently in the dressing until they're all shiny and delicious-looking. Chill the mixture before serving. If you can get some fresh basil, it's lovely chopped over the top of this salad.

CABBAGE AND BEAN SALAD

1 tablespoon wine vinegar
3 tablespoons salad oil
1 teaspoon sugar
½ teaspoon dry mustard
sea salt
freshly ground black pepper
1 tablespoon chopped fresh herbs
12 oz (350 g) white cabbage, finely shredded
2 sticks celery, chopped
½ green pepper, de-seeded and chopped
2 carrots, grated
2-3 tablespoons sultanas, washed and drained
4 oz (125 g) beans, any firm type, soaked, cooked and drained

SERVES 4

Put the vinegar, oil, sugar, mustard and some sea salt and freshly ground black pepper into a bowl and mix them together, then add all the other ingredients and stir them gently, so that they all get coated with the dressing. This is nice served with wholewheat rolls and some curd cheese.

CANNELLINI, APPLE AND CELERY SALAD

Actually you could use any white beans for this salad, but cannellini are nice because of their size and shape.

4 oz (125 g) cannellini beans
3 tablespoons oil
1 tablespoon lemon juice
sea salt
freshly ground black pepper

1 celery heart
2 eating apples
2 tablespoons raisins, washed and drained

SERVES 2-3

Prepare and cook the beans as usual; drain. Mix together the oil, lemon juice and some sea salt and freshly ground black pepper and add this to the beans, mixing gently. Wash and slice the celery; wash the apples and peel them if the skin is tough, then cut them into dice, discarding the core. Add the celery and apples to the beans, along with the raisins. Turn it gently with a spoon before serving so that everything gets mixed together and coated with the dressing.

CHICK PEA, APPLE AND LEEK SALAD

4 oz (125 g) chick peas
2 eating apples
1 tablespoon lemon juice
1 tablespoon oil
1 medium leek
1 tomato

sea salt
freshly ground black pepper

To serve:
crisp lettuce leaves

SERVES 3

Prepare and cook the chick peas as usual, then drain them. Wash the apples and peel them if they look as if they need it; then cut them into smallish dice, discarding the core. Add the apples to the chick peas, together with the lemon juice and oil. Wash the leek carefully, then cut it into thin rings, using the white part and as much of the green as possible; dice the tomato. Add the leek and tomato to the chick pea mixture. Season with sea salt and freshly ground black pepper. Serve the salad on a base of crisp lettuce leaves.

CHICK PEA NIBBLES

These puffy, garlic-flavoured chick peas always seem to go down well with drinks, but you can also serve them as the protein part of a light meal, accompanied by a dollop of mayonnaise, some sliced lemon and a crisp salad, in which case the quantity I've given would probably serve two people.

4 oz (125 g) chick peas
4 tablespoons wholewheat self-
   raising flour
1 clove garlic, crushed

sea salt
freshly ground black pepper
1 oz (25 g) butter
2 tablespoons oil

Prepare, cook and drain the chick peas as usual. Mix together the wholewheat self-raising flour and garlic; season with sea salt and freshly ground black pepper. Toss the chick peas in the seasoned flour, coating them as well as you can. Heat the butter and oil in a frying pan and add the chick peas; sprinkle any remaining flour on top of them. Gently fry the chick peas, turning them frequently, until they're crisp and golden all over. Drain them on kitchen paper and serve immediately, while they're all crisp and light.

CHICK PEA SALAD

This Middle Eastern salad is good served with crisp lettuce leaves and some chilled natural yoghurt.

6 oz (175 g) chick peas
2 cloves garlic
2 tablespoons olive oil
2 tablespoons lemon juice
sea salt

freshly ground black pepper
1 small onion, peeled and
   sliced into rings
3 tablespoons chopped parsley

SERVES 4

Cover the chick peas with plenty of cold water and leave them to soak for 4-5 hours or overnight. Then drain them and rinse thoroughly under cold water. Cook the chick peas gently in fresh cold water until they're tender; drain them thoroughly.

Meanwhile, peel and crush the garlic, put it into a medium-sized bowl and mix in the olive oil, lemon juice and some sea salt and freshly ground black pepper; add the drained chick peas (which can still be hot) and turn them in the dressing. Add the onion and parsley and leave the mixture to get cold. Check seasoning; serve cold or chilled.

CHICK PEA AND SPINACH
SALAD WITH YOGHURT

There's a lovely contrast of texture and colour in this Middle Eastern salad: firm golden chick peas against soft, bright green spinach, and smooth, creamy white yoghurt.

1 lb (450 g) spinach
6 oz (175 g) chick peas, cooked and drained
6 tablespoons olive oil
2 tablespoons wine vinegar
sea salt

freshly ground black pepper
¼ pint (150 ml) natural yoghurt
1-2 tablespoons chopped parsley

SERVES 4-6 AS A STARTER,
2-3 AS A SALAD MEAL

Thoroughly wash the spinach; cook it without extra water until it's tender, then cool, drain and chop it. Add the chick peas to the cooled spinach, together with the olive oil, vinegar and a good seasoning of sea salt and freshly ground black pepper. Mix well together, being careful not to break up the chick peas, then chill the salad until required.

To serve, arrange the spinach and chick pea mixture on a plate and spoon the natural yoghurt on top. Sprinkle with chopped parsley. Some thin buttered brown bread goes well with this.

If you want a crunchier texture, try adding some raw onion rings to the salad mixture; it's also nice with a flavouring of crushed garlic.

CONTINENTAL LENTIL AND MUSHROOM PÂTÉ

This curiously pleasant mixture can be served as part of a salad, piled on crisp lettuce leaves, sprinkled with a little olive oil and some onion rings and surrounded by wedges of hard-boiled egg; or, in smaller portions on individual dishes, it makes a delicious starter. Alternatively it can be served in a pâté dish, with Melba toast and butter, or thin brown bread and butter. It also makes a good sandwich filling, with or without the addition of thin slices of crisp raw onion or cucumber, tomato or other salad ingredients. Altogether rather a useful mixture, and not difficult to make, although I usually try to cook the lentils with another batch (or cook more and save the rest for something else) as it seems rather a small quantity to cook on its own.

4 oz (125 g) continental lentils
2 oz (50 g) button mushrooms
1 clove garlic
1½ oz (40 g) butter
1 tablespoon chopped parsley
sea salt
freshly ground black pepper
2-4 teaspoons lemon juice

SERVES 2 AS A SALAD MEAL,
4-6 AS A STARTER, PÂTÉ OR SANDWICH FILLING

Soak, drain, rinse and cook the lentils in the usual way until
very tender and beginning to disintegrate. Drain off any extra
liquid (it won't be needed for this recipe, but keep it for a gravy
or soup or something as it's full of flavour and nourishment).
Wipe the mushrooms and chop them up fairly finely; crush the
garlic. Melt the butter in a small saucepan and fry the mushrooms and garlic for 2-3 minutes, then remove them from the
heat and mix in the lentils and parsley. Season with sea salt,
freshly ground black pepper and lemon juice. Chill before
using.

CONTINENTAL LENTIL SALAD

This popular Mediterranean salad is one of the simplest, but
also one of the best. It's lovely on a hot day, served really cold,
with a crisp lettuce salad and an iced drink.

8 oz (225 g) continental
  lentils
olive oil
sea salt
freshly ground black pepper
1 onion, peeled and sliced into
rings

To serve:
hardboiled egg wedges
lemon slices

SERVES 4

Soak the lentils for a couple of hours or so in cold water, then drain and rinse them and cook gently in fresh cold water until they're tender. Drain the lentils well. Add to the hot lentils as much olive oil as they will take, then season the mixture with sea salt and freshly ground black pepper, cool and chill it. Just before serving, mix in the onion rings. Garnish with the wedges of egg and the lemon slices, and hand round extra olive oil and thin slices of brown bread and butter.

CREAMY BUTTER BEAN DIP

This is nice with a crisp salad or garlic bread; it's also good with sliced tomato and onion as a sandwich filling.

4 oz (125 g) butter beans
1 clove garlic, crushed
1 tablespoon olive oil
sea salt
freshly ground black pepper

To serve:
paprika pepper
black olives

SERVES 2 AS A SALAD,
4 AS A STARTER

Soak the butter beans as usual, then cook them in fresh water until they're very tender; drain. Mash the butter beans thoroughly with a fork or pass them through a mouli-légumes if you want a really smooth texture. Beat the garlic and oil into the butter beans and add sea salt and freshly ground black pepper to taste. Chill.

I think this looks attractive served forked up into a cone shape on a flat plate, sprinkled with paprika pepper and garnished with a few black olives. Some crisp lettuce leaves and watercress sprigs tucked round the edge look nice, too, and really turn it into a light meal.

CURRIED LENTIL AND PINEAPPLE SALAD

2 cloves garlic, crushed
1 medium-sized onion, peeled and chopped
6 tablespoons oil
1 tablespoon curry powder
8 oz (225 g) split red lentils
½ pint (275 ml) water
15 oz (425 g) pineapple pieces, drained and chopped
1 small green pepper, de-
seeded and chopped
1 tablespoon wine vinegar
sea salt
freshly ground black pepper

To serve:
lettuce leaves
a few onion rings
slices of tomato

SERVES 4

Fry the garlic and onion in half the oil in a medium-sized saucepan for 5 minutes, then add the curry powder and the split red lentils (washed and drained) and fry for a further 4-5 minutes, stirring often to prevent sticking. Mix in the water and let the mixture cook very gently for 20-30 minutes after which the lentils should be tender in texture and beige-gold in colour and all the water absorbed. Remove the saucepan from the heat and add the pineapple, green pepper, vinegar, remaining oil and sea salt and black pepper. Cool, then chill the salad and serve it piled up on lettuce leaves and garnished with slices of tomato and raw onion rings. Alternatively, it's very nice served scattered with desiccated coconut and garnished with sliced banana rings which have first been tossed in a little lemon juice to prevent them from discolouring.

CURRIED LENTIL SPREAD

This is a good mixture for sandwiches or little savoury biscuits.

4 oz (125 g) split red lentils	1 oz (25 g) butter
⅓ pint (200 ml) water	2 teaspoons curry powder
1 small onion, peeled and finely chopped	sea salt
	freshly ground black pepper

Wash the lentils and cook them in the water until they're tender and have absorbed all the water (20-30 minutes), then mash them roughly with a fork. Fry the onion in the butter until it's tender, then add the curry powder and fry for another 1-2 minutes. Blend this mixture into the cooked lentils to make a fairly smooth paste, then season to taste and leave the spread to get cold before using it.

CURRIED RICE AND CHICK PEA RING

This looks very attractive when it's finished (although it's easy to do), and is a useful dish for a party.

8 oz (225 g) long grain brown
rice
¾ pint (400 ml) water
1 teaspoon sea salt
2 large onions, peeled and
chopped
4 tablespoons oil
4-6 teaspoons curry powder
2 crisp eating apples
2 bananas
juice of ½ lemon

4 oz (125 g) raisins
6-8 tablespoons mayonnaise
(see page 91)
8 oz (225 g) chick peas, soaked,
rinsed, cooked and drained

To serve:
1 small red pepper, sliced into
thin rings, seeds removed
a little chopped parsley
½ bunch watercress

SERVES 6

Wash and pick over the rice, put it into a heavy-based saucepan with the water and sea salt and bring it up to the boil. Then
put a lid on the saucepan, turn the heat down, and leave the
rice to cook very gently for 45 minutes.

Fry the onion in the oil with the curry powder for 10
minutes until soft but not browned; add half to the cooked rice.
Peel and dice the apples and bananas and toss them in the
lemon juice; cover the raisins with a little boiling water and
leave on one side for 10 minutes, then drain them and add to
the rice with the apple and banana. Taste the rice mixture, and
season it as necessary. Press the rice mixture into an oiled 2
pint (1 l) ring mould and leave it to cool.

Stir the remaining onion and curry into the mayonnaise and
and then add the chick peas; season.

To assemble the dish, turn the rice ring out on to a large
serving dish and pile the chick pea mayonnaise into the centre.
Arrange the red pepper rings around the top of the rice ring,
sprinkle the chick pea mayonnaise with chopped parsley, and
tuck some sprigs of fresh, bright green watercress around the
outside edge of the ring. A salad of bright orange grated
carrots goes well with this.

FLAGEOLET AND AVOCADO SALAD

I'm particularly fond of this salad because its colours are so pleasing: pale green flageolet beans, yellow-green avocado and lettuce, dark green chives. (It also tastes good, by the way!)

4 oz (125 g) flageolet beans	sea salt
3 tablespoons oil	freshly ground black pepper
1 tablespoon white wine vinegar	1 ripe avocado pear
	a few crisp lettuce leaves
¼ teaspoon dry mustard	2 tablespoons chopped chives

SERVES 2 AS A SALAD MEAL,
4 AS A STARTER

Prepare and cook the beans as usual, then drain and cool them. Mix the oil with the vinegar, mustard and some sea salt and freshly ground black pepper, and add to the beans. Halve the avocado pear and gently remove the skin and the stone, then slice the flesh and add it to the beans. Turn the mixture gently, so that everything gets coated with the dressing, then serve it spooned on top of the lettuce leaves and sprinkled with the chopped chives.

FLAGEOLET AND
BUTTON MUSHROOM SALAD

1 clove garlic, crushed
3 tablespoons oil
1 tablespoon lemon juice
sea salt
freshly ground black pepper
4 oz (125 g) flageolet beans,
soaked, cooked, drained and
cooled
6 oz (175 g) very fresh white
button mushrooms
1 tablespoon chopped parsley

SERVES 2 AS A SALAD,
4 AS A STARTER

First of all make a dressing by mixing together the garlic, oil,
lemon juice and some sea salt and freshly ground black pepper.
Pour this dressing over the beans and mix them well, so that
they're all coated with it. Wash the mushrooms, then slice them
fairly finely and stir them into the bean mixture, together with
the chopped parsley. Check the seasoning, then chill the salad.

FLAGEOLET AND
SPRING ONION SALAD

4 oz (125 g) flageolets
1 tablespoon lemon juice
3 tablespoons olive oil
sea salt
freshly ground black pepper
6-8 large spring onions,
washed, trimmed and sliced

To serve:
crisp lettuce leaves

**SERVES 2 AS A SALAD,
4 AS A STARTER**

Soak and cook the beans as usual, then drain them well. Mix together the lemon juice, olive oil and a seasoning of sea salt and freshly ground black pepper. Pour this dressing over the beans (you can do this while they're still warm or you can use cold beans). Add the chopped spring onions and stir the mixture so that everything is well mixed. Cool the salad if necessary; serve it chilled and spooned over crisp lettuce leaves.

HARICOT BEAN AND GARLIC SPREAD

This makes a pleasant sandwich filling and is also good on little cocktail biscuits, decorated with small pieces of olive, etc. The basic mixture can be varied in a number of ways.

4 oz (125 g) haricot beans, cooked until tender, then cooled
1 oz (25 g) soft butter

1 clove garlic, crushed
a few drops of lemon juice
sea salt
freshly ground black pepper

Mash the beans to a smooth paste with a fork, then gradually blend in the butter, garlic and lemon juice. Season well with sea salt and freshly ground black pepper.

VARIATIONS

HARICOT BEAN AND PARSLEY SPREAD

Omit garlic from the recipe and add instead 2 tablespoons of chopped fresh parsley.

HARICOT BEAN AND FRESH HERB SPREAD

Instead of the garlic add 2 tablespoons of chopped fresh herbs: parsley, chives, tarragon, mint, fennel or lovage, whatever is available.

HARICOT BEAN AND OLIVE SPREAD

Make as above, leaving out the garlic and using instead 4-6 black olives, stoned and mashed to a smooth paste.

HARICOT BEAN AND HERB SALAD

You can really use any fresh green herbs for this salad: parsley and chives, of course, and any others available – mint, lovage, tarragon, basil, lemon balm, fennel and dill are all good.

8 oz (225 g) haricot beans	freshly ground black pepper
1 tablespoon wine vinegar	¼ teaspoon mustard
3 tablespoons oil	2-3 tablespoons fresh green
sea salt	herbs

SERVES 4-6 AS A STARTER,
3-4 AS A SALAD MEAL

Soak, cook and drain the beans as usual. Mix up a dressing, using the vinegar, oil, sea salt, freshly ground black pepper and mustard, and pour this over the beans. (You can do this while the beans are still warm.) Add the green herbs and mix well. Leave to cool, stirring the mixture from time to time so that all the flavours blend well together. Serve the salad nice and cold.

HARICOT BEAN SALAD, GRECIAN STYLE

This is a deliciously rich-tasting bean salad and is good with warm crusty rolls and a bowl of crisp lettuce and watercress.

8 oz (225 g) haricot beans	¼ pint (150 ml) water
8 tablespoons olive oil *or* half olive, half vegetable oil	juice of 1 lemon
2 cloves garlic, crushed	1 onion, peeled
1 teaspoon sea salt	freshly ground black pepper
2 teaspoons tomato purée	
2 sprigs thyme	*To serve*:
1 bayleaf	chopped parsley

SERVES 4

Soak the beans for a couple of hours or so, then drain and rinse them and cook them in plenty of water until nearly tender; drain. Heat the oil in a good-sized saucepan, add the beans and cook them very gently for about 10 minutes, then stir in the garlic, sea salt, tomato purée, thyme, bayleaf and water (you can use some of the water in which the beans were cooked) and simmer gently, without a lid, until the liquid has reduced to a thick, terracotta-coloured sauce and the beans are tender. Cool, then add the lemon juice and the onion, sliced into thin rounds. Season with more sea salt and freshly ground black pepper if necessary. Chill the salad and serve it sprinkled with chopped parsley.

HUMMUS

Eaten throughout the Middle East, this creamy dip is, in my opinion, one of the best pulse dishes. It's useful as part of a salad meal, as a spread or 'dip', as a sandwich filling or unusual starter. It's also extremely rich in protein and calcium.

4 oz (125 g) chick peas
1-2 cloves garlic, crushed
2 tablespoons lemon juice
2 tablespoons tahini (sesame cream, from health shops)
4 tablespoons olive oil

sea salt

To serve:
paprika pepper
lemon wedges

**SERVES 4 AS A STARTER,
2 AS A SALAD MEAL**

Soak, rinse and drain the chick peas, then cook them until they're tender and drain them, reserving the cooking water. Put the chick peas into the liquidizer goblet, together with 4-5 tablespoons of the cooking water, the garlic, lemon juice, tahini and half the olive oil, and liquidize until smooth, adding a little more cooking water to thin the mixture if necessary. Season carefully with sea salt. Chill the mixture.

To serve the hummus, spoon it on to a flat dish, smooth then fork over the top and pour the remaining olive oil gently over the top of the hummus; sprinkle it with paprika and garnish with lemon wedges.

LENTIL AND TOMATO SPREAD

4 oz (125 g) split red lentils
⅛ pint (200 ml) water
1 oz (25 g) softened butter
1 tablespoon tomato purée

a few drops lemon juice
sea salt
freshly ground black pepper

Cook the lentils in the water for 20-30 minutes, until they're tender and there's no water left, then let them cool. Mash the butter, tomato purée, a few drops of lemon juice and some sea salt and freshly ground black pepper into the cooked lentils to make a smoothish paste. This is nice in sandwiches with some raw onion, chutney or sliced tomato.

VARIATION

LENTIL AND CHIVE SPREAD

Make this as above but leave out the tomato purée and add 1-2 tablespoons of chopped chives instead.

RED BEAN AND ORANGE SALAD

A salad, this, for a grey winter's day, because the vivid colour is such a tonic! It's useful when conventional salad vegetables are scarce or unobtainable.

6 oz (175 g) red kidney beans
1 heart of celery
4 large oranges
2 tablespoons oil

2 tablespoons chopped fresh
mint
sea salt
freshly ground black pepper

SERVES 4

Cover the kidney beans with water and leave to soak for several hours; then drain and rinse them. Put them into a saucepan with plenty of cold water and cook gently for about 1 hour, or until they're tender. Drain and cool them.

Wash and slice the celery; cut the peel and pith from the oranges and slice the fruit into thin rounds. Mix together the orange, celery, beans, oil and mint. Add sea salt and freshly ground black pepper to taste. Chill before serving.

RED BEAN SALAD

Simple and well known, but still one of the best bean salads. Here's my version which goes well with a bowl of lettuce and watercress.

6 oz (175 g) red kidney beans	$\frac{1}{4}$ teaspoon dry mustard
1 onion	$\frac{1}{2}$ teaspoon sugar
1 clove garlic	1 tablespoon tomato purée
1 tablespoon red wine vinegar	sea salt
3 tablespoons olive oil	freshly ground black pepper

SERVES 3-4

Soak, cook and drain the beans; peel and slice the onion and crush the garlic. Add the onion and garlic to the beans. Mix together the vinegar, oil, mustard, sugar, tomato purée and some sea salt and freshly ground black pepper and pour this over the bean mixture, stirring well. As with most bean salads, I think this is best served very cold and it's certainly worth making it in advance so that the flavours have time to blend.

RICE AND BEAN SALAD

You can use any beans for this salad, though I generally use red kidney beans because their bright colour makes the mixture look so attractive.

4 oz (125 g) red kidney beans
8 oz (225 g) long grain brown
   rice
¾ pint (400 ml) water
sea salt
8 oz (225 g) aubergine
1 clove garlic
1 large onion
2 tablespoons oil

1 red pepper
4 oz (125 g) mushrooms
8 oz (225 g) canned tomatoes
freshly ground black pepper
2 drops tabasco

To serve:
a little chopped parsley

SERVES 4-6

Soak the beans, cook them until they're tender, then drain
them. Wash and pick over the rice, put it into a saucepan with
the water and a teaspoonful of sea salt, bring it up to the boil
and cook it as usual, over a very gentle heat with a lid on the
saucepan, until it's just tender and all the water has been
absorbed – 45 minutes.

Wash the aubergine and cut it into small pieces; sprinkle
with sea salt and leave for 30 minutes so that the sea salt can
draw out any bitter juices, then squeeze and rinse the aubergine
and pat it dry with kitchen paper. Crush the garlic, peel and
chop the onion and fry them in the oil in a good-sized saucepan for 10 minutes, then add the prepared aubergine and cook
for a minute or two longer while you de-seed and chop the
pepper and wash and slice the mushrooms. Then add the
pepper and mushrooms to the saucepan, also the canned
tomatoes, and let everything cook for a further 10 minutes or
so.

Using a fork, mix together the cooked rice, the vegetables
and the beans; season with sea salt, freshly ground black pepper
and tabasco. Let the salad get quite cold and serve it sprinkled
with chopped parsley.

RUSSIAN RED BEANS WITH DAMSON SAUCE

This Russian dish has an unusual, sweet flavour which goes well with a crunchy salad of white cabbage.

8 oz (225 g) red beans
2 tablespoons damson jam
½ teaspoon red wine vinegar
1 clove garlic, crushed

sea salt
½ teaspoon dried basil
½ teaspoon ground coriander

Soak and cook the beans as usual, then drain them. Sieve the jam and put it into a small saucepan with the vinegar; cook them gently over a low heat until the jam has melted, then add the crushed garlic, a little sea salt and the basil and coriander. Remove from heat and add to the beans, stirring well so that all the beans get coated. Leave the beans for 2-3 hours, so that the flavours can blend, then serve them very cold.

THREE BEAN SALAD

This colourful salad is good served with hot rolls or garlic bread and another salad of fresh vegetables, such as tomatoes with onion, or lettuce and watercress. The chick peas and haricot beans can be cooked together, but it is best to cook the red beans separately or you will end up with a whole pan of pink beans! Other beans can be used, but choose ones which will keep their shape after cooking.

3 oz (75 g) red kidney beans
3 oz (75 g) chick peas
3 oz (75 g) haricot beans
½ teaspoon dry mustard
½ teaspoon caster sugar
2 tablespoons wine vinegar
6 tablespoons olive oil

2-3 tablespoons chopped fresh
  green herbs – parsley, mint,
  chives, tarragon, fennel –
  whatever is available
sea salt
freshly ground black pepper

SERVES 4

Soak the beans in separate bowls, then rinse them. Cook the red kidney beans in one saucepan and the chick peas and haricot beans together in another, with plenty of water, until they're tender, then drain them.

Put the mustard and sugar in a bowl, blend with a little of the vinegar, then add the rest of the vinegar and the oil. Pour this dressing over the beans – this can be done while they're still hot – and mix well, being careful not to break them up. Add the herbs and sea salt and freshly ground black pepper to aste and leave to get cold. Serve chilled.

Bakes and Casseroles

The recipes in this section range from thrifty wartime dishes such as lentil pie and haricot casserole, to the exotic Middle Eastern musakka'a, a colourful mixture of aubergines, peppers, tomatoes and chick peas, and a spicy red bean moussaka. There's also an easy lentil and spinach casserole, lentils with fennel and a shepherds' beany pie, as well as Boston baked beans.

Some of these dishes include complementary proteins – haricot bean casserole, red bean moussaka, the lentil slices – others, while representing good protein in their own right, can be made even more nourishing by being served with extra, complementary protein in the form of rice, bread or yoghurt, as this enables all the pulse protein to be utilized. Where this applies I've given suggestions with the recipe.

BAKED BUTTER BEANS AND CHEESE

Although this dish takes about 2 hours to cook, the actual preparation is quick and easy, and while it's cooking you can really forget about it.

12 oz (350 g) butter beans
1 onion, peeled and sliced
1 clove garlic, crushed

2 carrots, scraped and sliced
2 sticks celery, sliced
2 oz (50 g) butter

bouquet garni – a sprig each of parsley and thyme, and a bayleaf, tied together
unsalted stock
8 oz (225 g) canned tomatoes
2 tablespoons chopped parsley
sea salt

freshly ground black pepper
chilli powder

For the topping:
4 oz (125 g) grated cheese
dry crumbs

SERVES 4

Soak the butter beans as usual, then drain and rinse them. Fry the onion, garlic, carrots and celery in the butter in a large, heavy-based saucepan for 10 minutes, then stir in the beans and add the bouquet garni and enough unsalted stock to cover by about ½ inch (1 cm). Bring the mixture up to the boil, then put a lid on the saucepan, turn the heat down and leave to simmer very gently for about 1¼ hours, until the butter beans are tender. Check the level of the water from time to time and add more stock if necessary.

Preheat the oven to 375°F (190°C), mark 5. Remove bouquet garni from the cooked butter beans and add to the saucepan the tomatoes and chopped parsley; season with sea salt, freshly ground black pepper and a little chilli powder. Turn the mixture into a greased ovenproof dish and sprinkle with grated cheese and crumbs. Bake in the oven for about 30 minutes, until golden and crisp on top. This is lovely served with just a simply cooked green vegetable, and perhaps some potatoes too if you're catering for very hungry people.

BLACK EYED BEAN BAKE

A simple dish, but one that's popular with children, I find. A nice spicy tomato sauce goes well with it, or a tasty gravy.

12 oz (350 g) black eyed beans, soaked in plenty of water overnight
2 large onions, peeled and sliced
3 cloves garlic, crushed
3 tablespoons vegetable oil
½ teaspoon thyme
1 teaspoon marjoram

¾ pint (400 ml) water *or* unsalted vegetable stock
sea salt
freshly ground black pepper

For topping:
wholewheat breadcrumbs
2 oz (50 g) grated cheese

SERVES 4

Drain and rinse the beans. Fry the onions and garlic in the oil for 10 minutes, until the onion is tender, then add the beans, herbs and water. Simmer gently, until the beans are tender (about 30-45 minutes). Preheat the oven to 350°F (180°C), mark 4. Liquidize the bean mixture or pass it through a vegetable mill, then season it to taste with sea salt and freshly ground black pepper. Spoon it into a greased shallow ovenproof dish, sprinkle with the wholewheat breadcrumbs and grated cheese and bake in the oven for about 30 minutes, until the top is golden and crunchy.

BOSTON BAKED BEANS

'Boston runs to brains as well as beans and brown bread,' noted William Cowper Brann in the *Iconoclast, Beans and Blood*. Well, here's a recipe for the beans.

12 oz (350 g) haricot beans
1 large onion
1 tablespoon oil
1 teaspoon dry mustard
2 teaspoons black treacle
¼ pint (150 ml) tomato juice

(you can use the liquid from a can of tomatoes)
2 tablespoons tomato purée
2 teaspoons brown sugar
½ pint (275 ml) unsalted stock

SERVES 4

Soak, drain and rinse the beans, then cook them in fresh water until they're almost tender, and drain them again.

Set the oven to 275°F (140°C), mark 1. Peel and slice the onion. Heat the oil in a flameproof casserole and fry the onion for about 5 minutes, then add the rest of the ingredients and bring the mixture up to the boil. Cover the casserole and put it into the oven; cook for about 4 hours, stirring occasionally. These beans are lovely served with hunks of hot wholewheat bread, or garlic bread.

CONTINENTAL LENTIL
TOAD-IN-THE-HOLE

4 oz (125 g) continental lentils

4 tablespoons oil
1 onion, peeled and chopped
1 clove garlic, crushed
4 oz (125 g) mushrooms, washed and sliced
1 teaspoon thyme
sea salt

freshly ground black pepper

For the batter:
4 oz (125 g) self-raising wholewheat flour
½ teaspoon sea salt
2 eggs
½ pint (275 ml) milk

SERVES 4-6

Wash, soak, rinse and cook the lentils, then drain them.

Preheat the oven to 425°F (220°C), mark 7. Heat 2 tablespoons of the oil in a good-sized saucepan and fry the onion and garlic for 5 minutes, letting them brown lightly, then add

126

the mushrooms and fry for another 5 minutes. Stir in the continental lentils, thyme and sea salt and freshly ground black pepper to season; keep the mixture hot.

Put the remaining oil into the shallow baking tin in which you are going to cook the toad-in-the-hole, and heat in the oven.

Next, make the batter. Sift the wholewheat flour and sea salt into a bowl and tip in the residue of bran left in the sieve. Make a well in the middle and add the eggs and about a third of the milk; beat vigorously with a wooden spoon, gradually incorporating the rest of the milk; beat well.

Pour the batter straight into the sizzling hot fat, then quickly spoon the lentil mixture on top. Bake for 20-25 minutes, until risen and golden. With gravy, potatoes and vegetables, this makes a good cheap family meal.

FENNEL AND LENTIL AU GRATIN

This is one of my favourite pulse dishes; the flavour and texture of the fennel go curiously well with the lentils.

1 onion, peeled and chopped
1½ oz (40 g) butter
6 oz (175 g) split red lentils
¾ pint (400 ml) water or un-
    salted stock
1 bayleaf
juice of ½ lemon

sea salt
freshly ground black pepper
1 lb (450 g) fennel

For the topping:
a few dried crumbs
a little grated cheese

SERVES 3-4

Fry the onion in 1 oz (25 g) of the butter in a medium-sized saucepan for 5 minutes, then add the washed lentils and the water or stock and bayleaf and simmer them gently for 20-30 minutes, until the lentils are soft and golden-beige. Then remove the bayleaf and liquidize the lentil mixture, adding the lemon juice and sea salt and freshly ground black pepper to taste.

Preheat the oven to 375°F (190°C), mark 5. Wash and trim the fennel, reserving some of the leafy green pieces. Cut the white part into chunky pieces and cook in a little boiling salted water until just tender; drain well. Use the remaining ½ oz (13 g) butter to grease generously a shallow ovenproof casserole dish. Put the cooked fennel in the base of the dish and pour the lentil mixture evenly over the top. Chop up about a tablespoonful of the reserved fennel leaves and scatter them over the lentil mixture, then sprinkle with dried crumbs and grated cheese. Bake in the preheated oven for 30-40 minutes, until crunchy and golden on top and hot and bubbling underneath. For maximum utilization of protein, serve a protein-rich starter, such as stuffed eggs, or follow this dish with a milk-based dessert.

HARICOT BEAN AND VEGETABLE PIE

As it's quite time-consuming to cook the carrots, leeks and mashed potatoes specially for this dish, I try to organize things so that they get cooked as part of a previous day's meal and kept in the refrigerator until required. But in writing this recipe, I'm assuming we're starting from scratch.

6 oz (175 g) haricot beans

2 oz (50 g) butter *or* margarine

1 large onion, peeled and chopped

1 large clove garlic, crushed

¾ pint (400 ml) water *or* unsalted stock

2 tablespoons tomato purée

½ teaspoon dried basil

sea salt

freshly ground black pepper

a little sugar

1½ lb (700 g) potatoes, peeled

1 lb (450 g) carrots, scraped and diced

1 lb (450 g) leeks, cleaned and sliced

a little milk

4 oz (125 g) grated cheese

SERVES 4

Soak the beans as usual, then drain and rinse them. Melt two-thirds of the butter in a medium-sized saucepan and fry the onion for about 10 minutes, then add the drained beans, garlic and water or stock. Bring up to the boil, then let it simmer gently for about 1 hour, until the beans are soft and the liquid reduced to a thick sauce. Stir in the tomato purée and season with basil, sea salt, freshly ground black pepper and a little sugar if necessary.

Meanwhile, cook the potatoes, carrots and leeks; drain. (The carrots and leeks can be cooked in the same saucepan.) Preheat oven to 375°F (190°C), mark 5. Mash the potatoes, using the remaining butter or margarine, a drop of milk and sea salt and freshly ground black pepper to taste.

Grease a shallow ovenproof casserole dish and put the leeks and carrots in the base; pour the bean mixture on top, sprinkle with most of the grated cheese, then spread the mashed potato on top. Fork over the top of the potato and sprinkle with the remaining cheese. Bake for 30-40 minutes, until piping hot and crispy and golden on top. It's nice served with a green vegetable like spinach or broccoli.

HARICOT AND ONION CASSEROLE

This is a wartime recipe which I've adapted slightly. It's very thrifty but surprisingly good to eat.

8 oz (225 g) haricot beans
sea salt
freshly ground black pepper
1 lb (450 g) onions
¾ pint (400 ml) water
approx. ½ pint (275 ml) milk
2 oz (50 g) margarine
2 oz (50 g) flour

2 oz (50 g) grated cheese
½ teaspoon dry mustard
8 oz (225 g) canned tomatoes, chopped

To finish:
a few dried crumbs
a little margarine

SERVES 4

Soak, drain and rinse the beans, then cover them with water and let them simmer gently for about 1 hour, or until tender. Drain; season with sea salt and freshly ground black pepper.

Preheat oven to 375°F (190°C), mark 5. Peel and slice the onions and cook them gently in the water until they're tender, then drain them, reserving the water and making it up to 1 pint (550 ml) with the milk. Melt the margarine in a saucepan and add the flour; when it 'froths' remove the saucepan from the heat and stir in the milk and onion water. Return the saucepan to the heat, stirring all the time for 3 minutes, until the sauce has thickened. Add the grated cheese, dry mustard, sea salt and freshly ground black pepper to taste.

Put the beans into a shallow greased casserole dish and arrange the tomatoes on top; season with sea salt and freshly ground black pepper. Put the onions on top of the tomatoes and season again; finally pour the sauce evenly over the onions.

Scatter a few crumbs over the top, dot with margarine and bake for 30-40 minutes. Serve with potatoes and a green vegetable.

LENTIL AND EGG BAKE

Another example of the excellent marriage of pulses with hardboiled egg. In this recipe, complementary protein is also present in the form of the wholewheat breadcrumbs, so it's very nutritious.

¼ pint (150 ml) vegetable oil
2 large cloves garlic, crushed
12 oz (350 g) fresh wholewheat breadcrumbs
1½ teaspoons dried thyme
8 oz (225 g) continental

lentils, soaked, cooked and well drained
freshly ground black pepper
sea salt
6 hardboiled eggs

SERVES 4-6

Set oven to 350°F (180°C), mark 4. Heat the oil in a large saucepan and add the garlic, wholewheat breadcrumbs and thyme. Fry them all in the oil, stirring continuously, until the breadcrumbs are crisp and lightly browned. Remove the saucepan from the heat and take out about a third of the breadcrumbs. Then mix the drained, cooked lentils with the rest of the breadcrumbs in the saucepan. Season well with freshly ground black pepper and sea salt.

Grease a shallow ovenproof dish and cover the base with half the lentil and wholewheat breadcrumb mixture. Shell and slice the hardboiled eggs and place them in a layer on top of the lentils and breadcrumbs, then spread the remaining lentil and breadcrumb mixture on top to cover them. Scatter with the reserved fried breadcrumbs. Bake in the oven for about 30 minutes, to heat everything through. A juicy tomato salad is lovely with this.

LENTIL AND MUSHROOM SLICE

6 oz (175 g) split red lentils
12 fl oz (350 ml) unsalted stock or water
1 large onion
6 oz (175 g) mushrooms
1 oz (25 g) butter

1 tablespoon chopped parsley
4 oz (125 g) grated cheese
1 egg
sea salt
freshly ground black pepper

SERVES 4

Put the lentils into a saucepan with the stock or water and simmer them gently until the lentils are soft and golden and all the liquid has been absorbed. Set oven to 375°F (190°C), mark 5.

Peel and chop the onion; wipe and slice the mushrooms. Melt the butter in a medium-sized saucepan and fry the onion and mushrooms together for about 10 minutes. Add the mushrooms and onion to the lentils, together with the parsley, grated cheese and egg. Mix well and season to taste with sea salt and freshly ground black pepper. Spread the mixture into a well-greased swiss roll tin (or similarly shaped casserole dish) and bake for about 35 minutes, until set and golden brown. Serve cut in slices, with a good spicy tomato sauce, buttery potatoes and cooked vegetables.

LENTIL PIE

Another economical wartime dish which I find is very popular with children, especially if they have it with fried potatoes and are allowed a free hand with the tomato ketchup! It's also nice with parsley sauce and slices of lemon.

6 oz (175 g) split red lentils	1 tablespoon chutney
1 large onion	sea salt
12 oz (350 g) mashed potatoes	freshly ground black pepper
1 tablespoon chopped parsley	½ oz (13 g) margarine

SERVES 4

Wash the lentils; peel and chop the onion. Put them into a saucepan with enough water to cover and cook gently until the lentils are tender and the water absorbed (20-30 minutes), then mash them lightly with a fork or potato masher. (The original recipe says 'pass through a sieve', but I think this is unnecessary.) Preheat oven to 400°F (200°C), mark 6. Beat the mashed potatoes into the cooked lentils, together with the parsley, chutney and sea salt and freshly ground black pepper to taste. Put the mixture into a shallow greased dish, smoothing then forking over the top. Melt the margarine and pour it over the top of the lentil mixture. Bake in the oven for about 20 minutes, until crisp and browned. (Alternatively, this can be cooked under a moderate grill if more convenient.)

LENTIL AND SPINACH CASSEROLE

The marriage of lentils and spinach is a particularly pleasing one, and this is a nice easy casserole to make.

8 oz (225 g) split red lentils   and sliced
1 pint (550 ml) water   sea salt
2 lb (1 kg) spinach   freshly ground black pepper
½ oz (13 g) butter   3-4 oz (75-100 g) grated
8 oz (225 g) tomatoes, peeled   cheese

SERVES 4

Cook the lentils in the water until they're soft, and pale in colour. Meanwhile wash the spinach carefully, then cook it in a dry saucepan for 7-10 minutes, until it's tender. Drain off the excess liquid and chop the spinach, then season it with sea salt and freshly ground black pepper. Preheat the oven to 375°F (190°C), mark 5.

Use the butter to grease a shallow ovenproof dish generously, then put the spinach in the base and arrange the tomatoes on top. Sprinkle with sea salt and freshly ground black pepper. Season the lentils and then pour them over the tomatoes and spread them to the edges of the dish; top with a layer of grated cheese. Bake in the oven for about 40 minutes. It's good with buttery noodles or new potatoes.

MUSAKKA'A

This colourful chick pea and aubergine casserole from the Middle East is lovely with fluffy brown rice or jacket-baked potatoes and a short-cooked green vegetable. If there's any over, it's surprisingly good served chilled, with crusty bread and some green salad.

5 oz (150 g) chick peas
2 lb (1 kg) aubergine
sea salt
2 large onions

¼ pint (150 ml) olive oil *or* vegetable oil *or* a mixture
14 oz (397 g) can tomatoes
freshly ground black pepper

SERVES 4

Soak the chick peas in cold water for several hours, then drain and rinse them, cover with fresh cold water, cook gently until they're tender, then drain them. Wash the aubergines and cut them into chunky pieces; put them in a colander, sprinkle with sea salt and place a plate and a weight on top. Leave for about 30 minutes to give the sea salt time to draw out any bitterness, then rinse the pieces and pat them dry on kitchen paper.

Set the oven for 400°F (200°C), mark 6. Peel and slice the onions and fry them in the oil in a large saucepan, then remove them with a draining spoon and fry the aubergine chunks in the oil until they're crisp and lightly browned. Put the aubergine pieces into a casserole dish, together with the oil in which they were cooked, the onion, chick peas, tomatoes and a good seasoning of sea salt and freshly ground black pepper. Cover the casserole and bake it in the oven for 40-60 minutes.

RED BEAN MOUSSAKA

This recipe was given to me by a friend, and I think it's very tasty, though I wouldn't try serving it to a Greek!

1 large aubergine	½ teaspoon cinnamon
sea salt	3-4 tablespoons red wine
1 large onion, peeled and chopped	8 oz (225 g) red kidney beans, soaked, cooked and drained
1 clove garlic, crushed	
2 tablespoons cooking oil	*To finish*:
3 tomatoes, skinned and chopped (or canned)	1 egg
1 tablespoon tomato purée	¾ pint (400 ml) well-flavoured white sauce
freshly ground black pepper	3 oz (75 g) grated cheese

SERVES 4-6

Slice the aubergine into thin rounds, sprinkle with sea salt and leave for 30 minutes to draw out bitter juices, then rinse and dry the pieces. Set oven to 350°F (180°C), mark 4.

Fry the onion and garlic in the oil in a good-sized saucepan for about 5 minutes, but don't brown them, then add the tomatoes, tomato purée, a good grinding of pepper, the cinnamon and wine and let the mixture cook gently for another 5 minutes or so, before mixing in the beans, mashing them slightly as you do so. Add more sea salt and freshly ground black pepper to taste if necessary.

Beat the egg into the white sauce; grease a shallow casserole dish. Put half the aubergine slices into the base of the dish, cover them with half the bean mixture and then half the white sauce. Repeat the layers, ending with the sauce, then sprinkle the top with the grated cheese. Bake the moussaka in the oven for about 1 hour. Serve with a cooked green vegetable or green salad.

SHEPHERDS' BEANY PIE

It's not essential to pass the cooked beans through a vegetable mill, but personally I think black eyed beans are much nicer in this type of dish if they've been puréed.

12 oz (350 g) black eyed beans
2 tablespoons vegetable oil
1 large onion, peeled and chopped
1 clove garlic, crushed
2 oz (50 g) mushrooms, wiped and chopped
8 oz (225 g) canned tomatoes
1 tablespoon tomato purée

1 tablespoon chopped parsley
1 teaspoon mixed herbs
sea salt
freshly ground black pepper

For topping:
1½ lb (700 g) creamy mashed potato
2 oz (50 g) grated cheese

SERVES 4

Soak the black eyed beans, then drain and rinse them. Put them into a saucepan, cover with water and cook until tender, then drain and pass them through a vegetable mill.

Meanwhile, heat the oil in a medium-sized saucepan and fry the onion and garlic for about 5 minutes, then put in the mushrooms and go on cooking for another 4-5 minutes. Add the tomatoes, tomato purée, the sieved beans, parsley and mixed herbs and cook over a gentle heat for 10 minutes. Then season with sea salt and freshly ground black pepper.

Set the oven to 400°F (200°C), mark 6. Grease a shallow

ovenproof dish and put the bean mixture in the base. Spread the mashed potato evenly over the top, rough up the surface with a fork and sprinkle with grated cheese. Bake in the oven for 35-40 minutes, until golden brown and crispy.

SHEPHERDS' LENTIL PIE

8 oz (225 g) continental lentils
1 large onion, peeled and chopped
1 clove garlic, crushed
1 stick celery, chopped
1 large carrot, scraped and diced
4 oz (125 g) mushrooms, wiped and chopped
2 oz (50 g) margarine

½ teaspoon thyme
½ teaspoon marjoram
1 tablespoon tomato purée
sea salt
freshly ground black pepper
1½ lb (700 g) creamy mashed potato

To finish:
a little margarine

SERVES 4

Soak the continental lentils, then drain and rinse them. Put them into a saucepan, cover with cold water and simmer gently until tender. Drain off any excess liquid.

Set oven to 400°F (200°C), mark 6. Fry all the vegetables in the margarine in a large saucepan for 15 minutes, until they're tender, then add the lentils, herbs, tomato purée and sea salt and freshly ground black pepper to taste.

Grease a shallow ovenproof dish and spoon in the lentil mixture; spread with the mashed potato and rough up the top with a fork. Dot with a little margarine and bake in the oven for 30-40 minutes, until piping hot and golden brown.

TURNIP AND LENTIL PIE

This wartime dish sounds like economy food with a vengeance, but, served with a tasty gravy and apple sauce it's actually not at all bad, and of course it's lovely and cheap.

8 oz (225 g) split red lentils
¾ pint (400 ml) water
2 oz (50 g) margarine
12 oz (350 g) grated turnip
4 oz (125 g) wholewheat breadcrumbs

1 egg
sea salt
freshly ground black pepper

To finish:
a little margarine

SERVES 4

Put the lentils, water and margarine into a medium-sized saucepan and simmer them gently for 20-30 minutes until the lentils are tender and all the liquid absorbed. Preheat the oven to 400°F (200°C), mark 6.

Add the turnip, wholewheat breadcrumbs and egg to the cooked lentils and season very well with sea salt and freshly ground black pepper. Spoon the mixture into a well-greased shallow casserole dish and smooth the top. Dot with a little margarine and bake for 30-40 minutes, until the top is lightly browned. Serve with a cooked green vegetable and gravy – and crisp golden roast potatoes if you're catering for really hungry people.

Cutlets, Loaves, Rissoles and Rolls

The starchy texture of most cooked pulses makes them ideal for forming into cutlets, loaves, rissoles and rolls, and this is one of the best ways of preparing them. A lentil rissole can be very delicious, crisp on the outside, tender and moist within, lovely with a well-flavoured sauce. Lentil or bean loaves and rolls work well, too, and as they're done in the oven it means you can cook some crispy golden roast potatoes at the same time, to have with them, together with vegetables and a tasty gravy. Or, rissoles and rolls can be served Middle Eastern fashion, with a dollop of chilled natural yoghurt (see the salads section) or, in the case of the little chick pea balls (felafel), in a fold of bread.

When cooking pulses for cutlets, loaves, rissoles and rolls, it's important not to make them too wet and 'mushy'. Split peas and split red lentils should be cooked in just enough liquid to be absorbed during the cooking time; this means 2 fl oz (50 ml) water to every 1 oz (25 g) for unsoaked pulses and half that quantity of water for soaked ones. The other pulses can be drained after cooking, so the amount of water is not so critical, but do drain them well and if necessary dry them a little afterwards by stirring them in a saucepan over a moderate heat.

Another way of cooking split red lentils, if you're worried about getting them too soggy on the one hand or having them stick to the saucepan on the other, is to steam them. Put the required quantity into a bowl, add water just barely to cover them (or measure it out as described above) and place the bowl in the top of a steamer. They take about 30-45 minutes and it's a good idea to give them a stir from time to time, turning sides to middle, to help them cook evenly.

If you want a smooth-textured cutlet or roll, the pulses can be passed through a vegetable mill or puréed in a liquidizer, though I hardly ever do this except for the felafel mixture which, being made from the firm-cooking chick peas, doesn't hold together unless it's been puréed. Apart from this, unless you're using a very tough-skinned bean, like the British field bean, which I think always benefits from sieving, just mashing the pulses with a fork is enough because a bit of texture seems to improve the finished dish.

If there's time, I often put a rissole or cutlet mixture into the refrigerator for half an hour or so to chill before shaping it; this firms it up and makes the job easier. For coating the rissoles, an egg and water mixture – one egg beaten up with a tablespoonful of cold water – is ideal and less sticky than using all egg, and then the rissoles can be dipped in 100 per cent wholewheat flour or crisp dry crumbs, both of which give a good finish. Or, for a really crisp coating, dip the rissoles first into wholewheat flour, then into egg and finally into dry wholewheat breadcrumbs.

BEANY SCOTCH EGGS

If you use a lentil loaf mixture to encase the hardboiled eggs, you've got that very successful partnership of lentils and hardboiled eggs in a particularly attractive form.

continental lentil and walnut
  mixture (see page 156)
4 hardboiled eggs

To finish:

wholewheat flour
2 eggs, beaten with 2 tablespoons cold water
dried crumbs
fat for deep frying

SERVES 4

Make the loaf mixture and let it cool; shell the eggs, leaving them whole.

To cover the eggs, dip them first in wholewheat flour, then in the beaten egg, then press some of the lentil mixture round them so that they are each completely covered. Next dip the covered eggs into the beaten egg again and roll them in dried crumbs. Heat the deep fat to 325°F (160°C), mark 3 and fry the Scotch eggs until they're crisp and golden brown all over (about 10 minutes); drain them on kitchen paper. Serve the Scotch eggs cut in half, with salad and perhaps some pickles.

BUTTER BEAN AND TOMATO CUTLETS

A friend gave me this tasty recipe which I think may have been developed from a wartime one.

4 oz (125 g) butter beans
1 medium onion, peeled and chopped
2 oz (50 g) margarine
2 oz (50 g) dried wholewheat breadcrumbs *or* crumbled Weetabix
2 tablespoons tomato chutney
1 teaspoon lemon juice

1 egg
sea salt
freshly ground black pepper

To finish:
beaten egg
dried crumbs to coat
oil for shallow frying

SERVES 2-3

Soak and cook the butter beans until they're tender, then drain and mash them. Fry the onion in the margarine until it's tender, but not browned, then add it to the butter beans with all the other ingredients, seasoning the mixture well with sea salt and freshly ground black pepper. Shape into cutlets and coat in egg and wholewheat breadcrumbs. Fry the cutlets in hot shallow oil, then drain them well on kitchen paper. They're nice served with a tasty gravy or tomato sauce.

CHICK PEA FRITTERS IN SWEET AND SOUR SAUCE

I like chick peas best for this Chinese-style recipe, but there's no reason why you shouldn't use other beans if you prefer – haricot beans, butter beans or cannellini beans would all be suitable. Serve the fritters with noodles or plain boiled rice and a crisp salad made from lettuce heart and onion rings.

6 oz (175 g) chick peas

For the batter mixture:
4 oz (125 g) self-raising whole-wheat flour
¼ teaspoon sea salt
1 egg
1 tablespoon soy sauce
2 teaspoons vegetable oil
¼ pint (150 ml) water

For the sweet and sour sauce:
1 onion
2 tablespoons oil
1 small green pepper, de-seeded and finely chopped
1 tablespoon cornflour
½ teaspoon ground ginger
½ teaspoon dried mustard
½ pint (275 ml) stock
2 tablespoons tomato purée
8 oz (225 g) can pineapple pieces, drained
1 tablespoon wine vinegar
1 teaspoon sugar
sea salt
freshly ground black pepper

For frying:
deep or shallow oil

SERVES 4

Soak the chick peas in water, then rinse, cook and drain them as usual. Next make the batter. Sift the wholewheat flour and sea salt into a bowl, adding also the residue of bran which will be left in the sieve. Make a well in the centre, break in the egg and add the soy sauce, oil and water. Mix thoroughly until everything is blended, then beat well. Cover and leave to stand for 30 minutes or so if possible.

Meanwhile, make the sweet and sour sauce. Peel and finely chop the onion and fry it in a medium-sized saucepan for about 5 minutes, then put in the finely chopped green pepper and cook, covered, for a further 4-5 minutes. Stir in the cornflour, ground ginger and dry mustard, then gradually pour in the stock, stirring all the time. Bring the mixture up to the boil and stir until thickened, then mix in the tomato purée. Crush the pineapple pieces with a fork or chop roughly and add them to the sauce, together with the wine vinegar and sugar. Season with sea salt and freshly ground black pepper. Simmer gently for about 10 minutes, to allow everything to cook and for the flavours to blend. Leave on one side while you make the fritters, then reheat just before the fritters are finished.

Mix the cooked and drained chick peas into the batter. If you're going to deep fry the fritters, heat the oil to temperature 325°F (160°C), mark 3; drop spoonfuls of the chick pea batter into the oil a few at a time and remove them with a perforated spoon when they're done. Drain them well on kitchen paper. If you're going to shallow fry them, cover the base of a frying pan with a little oil, make it nice and hot and fry spoonfuls of the chick pea batter, turning them over when they're cooked underneath; drain well on kitchen paper.

Pile the chick pea fritters on to a heated serving dish and pour the sauce over them. Serve at once.

CHICK PEA AND POTATO CROQUETTES

These creamy croquettes are good served with a tomato sauce and a green vegetable.

6 oz (175 g) chick peas, soaked, cooked and drained
1 lb (450 g) potatoes, cooked, drained and mashed (not too wet)
1 clove garlic, crushed
½ teaspoon paprika pepper
2 tablespoons chopped parsley
sea salt

freshly ground black pepper

To finish:
wholewheat flour
1 egg, beaten with 1 tablespoon water
dry crumbs
shallow oil for frying

SERVES 4

Mash the chick peas roughly with a fork, then mix them with the mashed potato, crushed garlic, paprika pepper and parsley. Season with sea salt and freshly ground black pepper. Form the mixture into small croquettes and roll them in wholewheat flour. Then dip the croquettes first into beaten egg and then into dry crumbs; fry them in hot, shallow oil; drain well on kitchen paper.

FELAFEL

In the Middle East, chick peas are used for these spicy little fritters, and very good they are too. However, I have found that split peas also make good felafel, and they are of course cheaper. These will cook to a 'mush' so that they can be mashed rather than passed through a vegetable mill, which saves time. But only use as much water as will be absorbed during the cooking, or they will be too moist.

8 oz (225 g) chick peas	sea salt
1 large onion	freshly ground black pepper
1 teaspoon ground coriander	
1 teaspoon ground cumin	*To finish*:
good pinch of chilli powder	wholewheat flour to coat
1 clove garlic, crushed	oil to shallow fry

SERVES 4

Soak the chick peas in cold water for several hours, then drain, cover with fresh cold water and simmer gently until very tender – 1-2 hours. Drain the chick peas and pass them through a fairly fine blade on a vegetable mill (I use a mouli-légumes).

Peel and finely grate the onion and add it to the chick peas, together with the spices, garlic and sea salt and freshly ground black pepper to taste. If the mixture is rather soft, put it into the refrigerator for half an hour or so to firm up.

Form tablespoonfuls of the mixture into small, flat cakes, coat them well in wholewheat flour and then shallow fry them in hot oil until they're brown on both sides.

Felafel can be served Middle Eastern style with pitta bread, or, English style, with a garnish of lemon and parsley and seasonal vegetables. For the adventurous, I recommend them with the chilled yoghurt and garlic sauce on page 151.

GREEN PEA FRITTERS

These are really a cross between a fritter and a rissole. I usually pass the cooked peas through a vegetable mill to remove their outer skins which can be rather obtrusive, but this is not essential.

8 oz (225 g) dried whole green peas
1 tablespoon melted butter
2 eggs
4 oz (125 g) self-raising whole-wheat flour

¼ pint (150 ml) milk
sea salt
freshly ground black pepper

To finish:
oil for shallow frying

SERVES 4

Cover the peas with boiling water and leave them to soak for several hours, then drain and rinse them, put into a saucepan with more water and simmer until they're soft – about 45 minutes. Drain them if necessary, then pass them through a vegetable mill. Add the butter, eggs, wholewheat flour and milk to the pea purée and season the mixture with sea salt and freshly ground black pepper.

Heat a little oil in a frying pan and fry dessertspoonfuls of the mixture until crisp and brown, turning them so that both sides are cooked. Drain them well on kitchen paper.

These fritters are a good source of protein and I like to serve them with a tasty brown onion gravy and vegetables. Mint sauce also goes well with them.

LENTIL AND CHEESE CROQUETTES WITH TOMATO SAUCE

I find that these crisp, tasty little croquettes appeal even to those who don't think they like lentils! It's important to cook the lentils until they have absorbed all the water and are 'dry', or the mixture will be too moist. The flavouring can be varied according to taste; herbs such as sage are pleasant and so is a little cinnamon or curry powder.

12 oz (350 g) split red lentils
1¼ pints (700 ml) water
1 large onion, peeled and finely chopped
2 tablespoons oil
6 oz (175 g) grated cheese
½ teaspoon chilli powder
½ teaspoon dry mustard
½ teaspoon paprika pepper
sea salt
freshly ground black pepper

To finish croquettes:
wholewheat flour
1 egg, beaten with 1 tablespoon cold water
dry crumbs
oil for shallow frying

For the sauce:
1 small onion, peeled and chopped
2 cloves garlic, crushed
2 tablespoons oil
14 oz (397 g) can tomatoes
1 bayleaf
sea salt
freshly ground black pepper
a little sugar
pinch of chilli powder

SERVES 4

Wash the lentils and put them into a saucepan with the water. Simmer them for about 30 minutes, until they're tender and have absorbed all the water. Fry the onion in the oil until it's soft but not brown, then mix it in with the cooked lentils, together with the grated cheese, chilli powder, mustard, paprika and sea salt and freshly ground black pepper to taste.

Divide the mixture into eight or twelve pieces, roll each in wholewheat flour and form it into a croquette, then dip it first into the egg and then into the wholewheat breadcrumbs.

Fry the croquettes in hot, shallow oil and drain them well on kitchen paper. Serve them with the sauce. Buttery spaghetti, noodles or potatoes go well with this.

To make the sauce, fry the onion and garlic in the oil in a medium-sized saucepan for 10 minutes, then stir in the tomatoes and bayleaf. Let the mixture simmer, uncovered, for 10-15 minutes, until it's thick and purée-like. Season with sea salt, freshly ground black pepper, a little sugar and a pinch or so of chilli powder to taste.

LENTIL AND EGG CUTLETS

Continental lentils and hardboiled eggs are one of those great combinations, like basil and tomatoes and sage and onion. I particularly like them together in these crisp cutlets.

8 oz (225 g) continental lentils
½ pint (275 ml) water
1 large onion
2 oz (50 g) butter
4 hardboiled eggs
2 tablespoons finely chopped parsley

¼ teaspoon powdered mace or a little grated nutmeg
sea salt
freshly ground black pepper

To finish:
wholewheat flour to coat
oil for shallow frying

SERVES 4

Soak, drain and rinse the lentils as usual, then cover them with the water and cook them gently until they're soft and have absorbed the water. Meanwhile, peel and finely chop the onion and fry it in the butter for about 10 minutes until it's tender and golden brown. Peel and chop the hardboiled eggs and mix them in with the cooked lentils, together with the onion, parsley, mace or nutmeg and sea salt and freshly ground black pepper to taste. Let the mixture cool, then shape it into eight round cutlets and roll them in wholewheat flour. Fry the cutlets in hot, shallow fat until they're crisp on both sides;

drain them on kitchen paper.

These are lovely served with some plain or garlic mayonnaise or with yoghurt and a crunchy cabbage, carrot, green pepper and pineapple salad. Or serve them with creamy mashed potatoes, cooked vegetables and a good gravy.

LENTIL AND ONION RISSOLES
WITH MINT SAUCE

The sharpness of the sauce goes well with the lentils. Serve these rissoles with cooked vegetables and mashed potatoes for a complete meal.

12 oz (350 g) split red lentils
1¼ pints (700 ml) water
1 large onion, peeled and chopped
1 oz (25 g) vegetable margarine
1 egg
sea salt
freshly ground black pepper
1 tablespoon lemon juice

To finish:
wholewheat flour for coating
oil for shallow frying

For the sauce:
2 heaped tablespoons fresh chopped mint
1 tablespoon boiling water
1 tablespoon sugar
2 tablespoons cider vinegar *or* white wine vinegar

SERVES 4

Put the lentils into a good-sized saucepan with the water and cook them gently for about 30 minutes, until they're soft and pale. Fry the onion in the fat for 10 minutes, letting it brown lightly. Add the fried onion and the egg to the cooked lentils, mashing the lentils a bit as you do so. Flavour with sea salt,

freshly ground black pepper and lemon juice. Form the
mixture (which should be fairly stiff) into little rounds and roll
them in wholewheat flour. Fry them on both sides in hot,
shallow oil and drain them on kitchen paper. Serve them with a
sauce made by mixing together the mint, boiling water, sugar
and vinegar. I usually do this by whizzing them all in the
liquidizer for a minute or two and this means there's no need
to chop the mint: one can put in the whole sprigs with just any
tough stems removed.

LENTIL RISSOLES WITH YOGHURT SAUCE

I think these spicy rissoles are best with a chilled yoghurt
sauce, but you could serve them with a hot tomato or curry
sauce. In any case, they're good with lots of fluffy brown rice
and a green salad.

8 oz (225 g) split red lentils
¾ pint (400 ml) water
1 onion, peeled and finely
  chopped
2 tablespoons oil
½ teaspoon ground cumin
½ teaspoon ground coriander
½ teaspoon turmeric
1 egg
1 tablespoon lemon juice
sea salt

freshly ground black pepper

To finish:
wholewheat flour to coat
oil to shallow fry

For the sauce:
½ pint (275 ml) natural yoghurt
2 tablespoons chopped parsley
1 clove garlic, crushed

SERVES 4

Put the lentils and water into a medium-sized saucepan and
cook them for about 30 minutes, until the lentils are pale and

soft and all the water has been absorbed.

Fry the onion in the oil for about 10 minutes, until it's soft, then put in the spices and fry for a further 2-3 minutes. Add the onion and spices to the lentils, together with the egg, lemon juice and seasoning to taste. Mix it all together well, then form it into small rissoles and coat each one with wholewheat flour.

Heat a little oil in a frying pan and fry the rissoles until they're crisp, then drain them on kitchen paper and keep them warm.

Make the sauce by mixing together the yoghurt, parsley and garlic. Season with sea salt and freshly ground black pepper and serve with the rissoles.

SPICY CONTINENTAL LENTIL RISSOLES

These rissoles are good with some buttery noodles or brown rice and a well-flavoured curry or tomato sauce. They're also nice cold, with natural yoghurt, mango chutney and salad.

8 oz (225 g) continental lentils
½ pint (275 ml) water
2 tablespoons oil
1 large onion, peeled and chopped
1 large clove garlic, crushed
1 small green pepper, deseeded and chopped
1 teaspoon turmeric
1 teaspoon ground coriander

1 teaspoon ground cumin
¼-½ teaspoon chilli powder
sea salt
freshly ground black pepper

To finish:
1 egg, beaten with 1 tablespoon water
dried crumbs
shallow oil for frying

SERVES 3-4

Wash and soak the lentils as usual, then rinse them and put them into a saucepan with the water; simmer them gently until they're tender and have absorbed all the liquid – 30-45 minutes.

Meanwhile heat the oil in a medium-sized saucepan and fry the onion for 5 minutes or so, then add the garlic and green pepper and cook for a further 5 minutes; stir in the spices and let them cook for another minute or two. Add the fried vegetables and spices to the cooked lentils, season with sea salt and freshly ground black pepper and then leave the mixture to get cold. Form into small rissoles and dip them first into the beaten egg and then into dried crumbs. Fry the rissoles in shallow fat until they're crisp on both sides, then drain them on kitchen paper.

SOYA BEAN AND EGG CROQUETTES

There's no problem about protein here: these tasty little croquettes are as nutritious as any beef steak!

4 oz (125 g) soya beans, soaked, well rinsed, cooked until very tender and drained
1 onion, peeled and finely chopped
1 clove garlic, crushed
1 oz (25 g) butter
4 hardboiled eggs
2 oz (50 g) wholewheat breadcrumbs
1 tablespoon tomato purée

2 tablespoons chopped parsley
½ teaspoon ground mace
1 egg
sea salt
freshly ground black pepper

To finish:
wholewheat flour
beaten egg
dried crumbs
oil for shallow frying

SERVES 3-4

Mash the beans with a fork, just to break them up. Fry the
onion and garlic in the butter for 10 minutes, then remove
from the heat and stir in the beans. Shell the hardboiled eggs,
then chop them fairly finely and add them to the beans,
together with the wholewheat breadcrumbs, tomato purée,
chopped parsley, mace and egg. Mix well, then taste and
season. Form mixture into little croquettes, roll them in
wholewheat flour, then dip them into beaten egg and roll them
in dried crumbs. Fry the croquettes in hot, shallow oil and
drain them well on kitchen paper. They're nice with a spicy
tomato sauce.

VARIATION

Soya bean and walnut croquettes are good, too. Omit the egg
and use instead 4 oz (125 g) walnuts, pulverized in the liquidizer, and ½ teaspoon dried thyme. You may need to add a little
more liquid to the mixture (or don't use all the wholewheat
breadcrumbs).

SPLIT PEA CUTLETS WITH
APPLE RINGS

Fruit goes surprisingly well with pulses; here, there is also a
pleasant contrast of texture, soft apple rings against crisp
cutlets.

12 oz (350 g) yellow split peas
¾ pint (400 ml) water
1 large onion, peeled and chopped
1 oz (25 g) butter
½ teaspoon sage
pinch of ground cloves
1 egg
sea salt
freshly ground black pepper
a little lemon juice

To finish:
wholewheat flour
1 egg, beaten with 1 tablespoon water
dry crumbs
shallow oil for frying

For the apple rings:
2 medium-sized cooking apples
1 oz (25 g) butter
2 tablespoons oil

SERVES 4

Soak the split peas in water, then rinse them. Put them into a saucepan with the water and cook them until they're tender; drain if necessary and dry by stirring over a moderate heat for a minute or two.

Fry the onion in the butter in a large saucepan for 10 minutes, then add the sage, split peas, ground cloves and egg. Mix well, mashing the split peas a bit with the spoon, then season with sea salt and freshly ground black pepper and add a little lemon juice if you think the mixture needs it.

Shape the split pea mixture into 12 small cutlets on a floured board, then dip each in egg and dry crumbs; coat well. Fry the cutlets in hot shallow oil until they're crisp on both sides; drain them on kitchen paper and keep them warm.

To make the apple rings, peel the apples and remove the core using an apple-corer, keeping the apple whole. Then slice the apples into thin rings. Heat the butter and oil in a clean frying pan and fry the apple rings for a minute or two on each side to cook them through and brown them lightly. Serve the cutlets with the apple rings.

CONTINENTAL LENTIL AND WALNUT LOAF

People usually find it difficult to guess what this loaf is made from: the result is tasty and 'chewy' and of course it's packed with protein. It's nice served hot with roast potatoes, gravy and vegetables – a vegetarian-style Sunday lunch – or cold, with some mayonnaise or chutney.

6 oz (175 g) continental lentils

1 onion, peeled and chopped up small

1 large clove garlic, crushed

2 tablespoons oil

1 teaspoon dried thyme

4 oz (125 g) walnuts, ground or pulverized in the liquidizer

4 oz (125 g) wholewheat

breadcrumbs

1 tablespoon tomato purée

1 tablespoon chopped fresh parsley

1 egg

sea salt

freshly ground black pepper

To serve:

1 tomato, sliced

a few sprigs of parsley

SERVES 4-6

Soak the lentils for a few hours, then rinse them and put them into a saucepan with enough cold water to cover. Simmer gently for about 40 minutes, until they're tender, then drain off any liquid.

Prepare a 1 lb (450 g) loaf tin by putting a long strip of foil across the bottom and up the two narrow sides; grease it generously with butter. Set oven to 375°F (190°C), mark 5.

Fry the onion and garlic in the oil in a good-sized saucepan for 10 minutes until tender and lightly browned; stir in the thyme and fry for a few seconds, then remove the saucepan from the heat and add the lentils, walnuts, wholewheat bread-crumbs, tomato purée, parsley and egg. Mix well, then season with sea salt and freshly ground black pepper. Spoon the mixture into the prepared loaf tin and smooth the top. Cover with a piece of greased foil and bake in the oven for 1 hour. Leave the loaf to stand in its tin for a minute or two after removing it from the oven, then slip a knife round the edges of the loaf to loosen it and turn it out; strip off the foil. Garnish the top of the loaf with slices of tomato and a sprig of parsley.

MOCK GOOSE

This is a wartime recipe (slightly adapted) for a layered lentil loaf which no self-respecting goose would own! But it's quite good and tasty in its own right, especially if served with a well-flavoured gravy and some apple sauce.

6 oz (175 g) split red lentils
½ pint (275 ml) water
½ oz (13 g) margarine
1 tablespoon lemon juice
sea salt
freshly ground black pepper

For the stuffing:
1 large onion, peeled and
chopped
2 tablespoons oil
2 oz (50 g) soft wholewheat
breadcrumbs
1½ teaspoons dried sage

To finish:
a little margarine

SERVES 2-3

Wash the lentils and put them into a saucepan with the water; simmer them gently until they're cooked and all the water has been absorbed, then beat in the margarine, lemon juice and seasoning. Set oven for 400°F (200°C), mark 6.

For the stuffing, fry the onion in the oil for about 10 minutes, then take it off the heat and add the wholewheat breadcrumbs, sage and a seasoning of sea salt and freshly ground black pepper.

Put a layer of half the lentils into a greased 1 lb (450 g) loaf tin or casserole dish; spread the stuffing on top and then spoon in the remaining lentils and smooth the top. Dot with margarine and bake in the oven for 30-40 minutes, until the top is browned and crisp. It's good served with some crisp golden roast potatoes and cooked cauliflower.

SOYA LOAF

This is my adaptation of an American recipe that was given to me. It makes a tasty loaf, and of course it's very rich in protein.

6 oz (175 g) soya beans
1 large onion, peeled and chopped
2 cloves garlic, crushed
4 sticks celery, washed and chopped
2 oz (50 g) butter
2 tomatoes, peeled and chopped
2 tablespoons tomato purée
4 oz (125 g) wholewheat breadcrumbs
4 tablespoons chopped parsley
1 teaspoon dried thyme
1 egg
sea salt
freshly ground black pepper

To finish:
a little butter
dry crumbs

SERVES 4-5

Soak, rinse and cook the soya beans as usual – they will take about 4 hours to get really soft. Then drain and mash them. Preheat the oven to 375°F (190°C), mark 5.

Fry the onion, garlic and celery in the butter in a good-sized saucepan for about 15 minutes, until they're all tender, then add the tomatoes and tomato purée and cook gently for a further 5 minutes. Stir in the soya beans, wholewheat breadcrumbs, parsley, thyme and egg and season the mixture carefully with sea salt and freshly ground black pepper.

Grease a 1 lb (450 g) loaf tin very generously with butter, then coat with dried crumbs, which should stick to the butter. This will help the loaf to come out of the tin easily and make the outside nice and crisp. Spoon the soya mixture into the tin and smooth down the top. Cover with a piece of buttered foil and bake in the oven for 1 hour. Let the loaf stand for a minute or so, then slip a knife round the edges and turn it out on to a warm dish. Serve with roast potatoes, gravy and vegetables. Apple sauce goes well with it, too.

WARTIME BEAN ROAST

This is another of those abstemious wartime recipes which works very well, though I think the roast does need to be served with a good tasty sauce – a spicy tomato one, or a really well-flavoured gravy, perhaps.

8 oz (225 g) butter beans, soaked, rinsed and cooked as usual
2 oz (50 g) margarine
1 onion, peeled and chopped
4 oz (125 g) breadcrumbs
4-6 tablespoons strongly flavoured tomato or curry sauce
sea salt
freshly ground black pepper

To finish:
beaten egg and dried crumbs to coat
a little margarine

SERVES 4

Preheat the oven to 400°F (200°C), mark 6. Drain and mash the butter beans, but don't make them too smooth. Melt the margarine in a saucepan and fry the onion for about 10 minutes, until it's soft, then add it to the butter beans, together with the breadcrumbs and enough of the sauce to flavour and bind the mixture; season with sea salt and freshly ground black pepper. Then form the mixture into a roll and dip it first in beaten egg and then into dried crumbs. Put the roll on to a well-greased baking sheet and dot it with a little extra margarine. Bake for about 45 minutes in the oven, until the roll is browned and crisp. I think apple sauce goes well with this roast.

Pasta and Pancakes

You might think that the combination of pulses and pasta or pancakes would be definitely erring on the side of stodge, but, if the dish is well cooked, this is not the case, and in fact this combination is, in my opinion, one of the best.

Light, feathery pancakes wrapped round a moist, tasty bean mixture and topped with a cheese sauce, or succulent lasagne layered with a rich, wine-flavoured lentil purée make very tasty eating indeed. They are also extremely satisfying, bringing together, as they do, the two complementary proteins, pulse and wheat, not to mention the extra dairy proteins which are also included, so they provide excellent nourishment tastily and economically.

Incidentally, you will notice in the recipes that I suggest using wholewheat pasta, which is what I prefer, but if you don't like this, then substitute your own favourite variety. I must say I do like the buckwheat pasta, which you can get at health shops: it's quick to cook, light and has a lovely flavour.

Although the list of ingredients in these recipes may look a bit long and daunting, don't let this deter you. Usually these dishes can be made in several easy-going stages which can be fitted in with other tasks, so that with a little forward planning they are not really too irksome. Also, remember that unless you're catering for very hungry people, you don't really need to serve potatoes as well, so that's one job less, and mostly these dishes can be served with just a quickly cooked green vegetable or tossed green salad. They are nice washed down with a robust red wine, though, if you want to celebrate!

BASIC PANCAKE BATTER

I usually make this batter in a liquidizer, which is very labour-saving, but you can equally well use the traditional method.

4 oz (125 g) plain 81 per cent flour
¼ teaspoon sea salt
2 size 4 (standard) eggs
2 tablespoons vegetable oil

7 fl oz (200 ml) milk

For frying:
oil

MAKES 10-12 PANCAKES

It you're using the quick liquidizer method to make the batter, simply put all the ingredients into the goblet and blend at medium speed for 1-2 minutes to make a smooth, creamy batter. Or, for the traditional method, sift the flour and sea salt into a bowl, make a well in the centre and add the eggs, the oil, and about a third of the milk. Mix to a smooth consistency, gradually adding the remaining milk, then beat well for 1-2 minutes. Whichever method you use, leave the batter to stand for 30 minutes before using it, then beat it again lightly.

To fry the pancakes, set a small frying pan over a low heat and brush the inside with oil. When the pan is hot, pour in about 2 tablespoons of batter – enough to coat the bottom of the frying pan thinly – and swirl it round so that the base of the frying pan is covered. Fry for a minute or two, until the base of the pancake is cooked, then, using a palette knife or fish slice, quickly flip the pancake over to cook the other side. When that's done, lift out the pancake and put it on a plate while you make the rest. Brush the frying pan with oil before making each pancake, and pile them up on top of each other on the plate as they're done. I don't find there's any need to put pieces of greaseproof paper between the pancakes, as some people suggest, by the way: they don't seem to stick together. It is a good idea to keep an old pastry brush specially for oiling the frying pan, though, as the heat of the pan makes the bristles curl.

Pancakes freeze very well: simply wrap the pile of cooled pancakes in foil and put them in the freezer. When you want to use them, loosen the foil and let them thaw out naturally, or put the foil parcel in a low oven if you want to speed up the process. They will also keep for several days in an ordinary refrigerator.

CHILLI RED BEAN PANCAKES

It's up to you how 'hot' you make the chilli red bean filling for the pancakes, but I start with the smaller quantity of chilli powder and taste carefully!

For the pancakes:
basic pancake batter (see page 162)
oil for frying

For the filling and sauce:
6 oz (175 g) red kidney beans, soaked for several hours in cold water, then drained and rinsed
1 pint (550 ml) water
2 tablespoons oil

2 onions, peeled and chopped
2 cloves garlic, crushed
1 bayleaf
½ teaspoon oregano
14 oz (397 g) can tomatoes
1 tablespoon tomato purée
½-1 teaspoon chilli powder
sea salt
freshly ground black pepper

For the topping:
4 oz (125 g) grated cheese

SERVES 4

Use the pancake batter to make 10-12 thin pancakes: these can be made in advance if it's more convenient. Put the beans into a saucepan with the water and cook them gently until they're tender – about 1 hour – then drain them, reserving the cooking liquid.

Preheat the oven to 350°F (180°C), mark 4. Heat the oil in a medium-sized saucepan and fry the onion for 10 minutes, but don't let it get brown, then add the garlic, bayleaf, oregano, tomatoes, tomato purée and chilli powder and let it all simmer gently, uncovered, for about 15 minutes. Add half of this tomato mixture to the cooked beans, mashing them roughly, and seasoning with sea salt, freshly ground black pepper and, if necessary, more chilli powder to taste. Spread about 2 tablespoons of this bean mixture on each pancake, roll them up and place them side by side in a well-greased shallow ovenproof dish.

Mix the rest of the tomato mixture with the reserved bean liquor – there should be just under ¼ pint (150 ml). Season to taste, then pour this over the pancakes and sprinkle the top with grated cheese. Put the dish into the oven for about 30 minutes, to heat it through and brown the top. It's lovely served with buttery spinach or broccoli.

PANCAKES WITH FLAGEOLET, MUSHROOM AND ARTICHOKE HEART FILLING

I must admit this is rather an extravagant recipe, using two cans of artichoke hearts. But it's an example of pulses dressed up for a party, a special-occasion dish.

For the pancakes:
pancake batter (see page 162)
oil for frying

For the filling:
8 oz (225 g) flageolet beans,
    soaked for several hours in
    cold water
12 oz (350 g) button mush-
    rooms
2 cloves garlic
2 oz (50 g) butter

2 14 oz (397 g) cans artichoke
    hearts
6 oz (175 g) cream cheese
2 tablespoons chopped parsley
sea salt
freshly ground black pepper

To finish:
¾ pint (400 ml) well-flavoured
    cheese sauce (see page 62)
2 oz (50 g) grated cheese
a few dry crumbs

SERVES 6

Use the pancake batter to make 10 or 12 thin pancakes as usual;
stack them up in a pile on a plate and leave on one side while
making the filling.

Drain and rinse the flageolets and put them into a saucepan
with a good covering of cold water. Simmer them gently for
about 1 hour, until they're tender, then drain them. Preheat
oven to 350°F (180°C), mark 4.

Wipe and slice the mushrooms, peel and crush the garlic
and fry them together in the butter for 4-5 minutes, until the
mushrooms are tender. Drain and roughly chop the artichoke
hearts and add them to the mushrooms, together with the
cooked flageolets, cream cheese, parsley and seasoning; mix
well.

Spread the pancakes with the filling, then roll them up and
place them side by side in a shallow buttered casserole. Pour
the sauce over the pancakes and sprinkle the grated cheese and
crumbs on top. Bake the pancakes in the oven for 35-40
minutes until heated through and lightly browned on top.

PANCAKE GÂTEAU

This is quite a spectacular-looking dish, a 'gâteau' of light pancakes layered with three different mixtures, spinach, continental lentil, and tomato, topped with a creamy sauce. You can use different fillings if you like, but aim for contrasting colours, as they look so attractive when the 'gâteau' is sliced. You can make all the parts of the 'gâteau' separately in advance and the actual assembly only takes a matter of minutes.

For the pancakes:
basic pancake batter (see page 162)
oil for frying

Continental lentil filling:
4 oz (125 g) continental lentils, soaked in cold water overnight
1 large onion, peeled and chopped
1 large clove garlic, crushed
1 tablespoon oil
sea salt
freshly ground black pepper

Tomato filling:
1 large onion, peeled and chopped
1 clove garlic, crushed
1 tablespoon oil
14 oz (397 g) can tomatoes
½ teaspoon oregano

Spinach filling:
1½ lb (700 g) spinach
½ oz (13 g) butter
grated nutmeg

For the topping:
¾ pint (400 ml) well-flavoured cheese sauce (see page 62)

To serve:
1 tomato, sliced
a few sprigs of parsley

SERVES 4-6

Use the basic batter mixture to make 10 thin pancakes, piling them up on a plate as they're ready, then leaving them on one side while you make the fillings.

For the lentil filling, drain and rinse the lentils, then put them into a saucepan, just cover with water and cook gently until they're tender – 30-40 minutes. Drain off any excess liquid. Meanwhile fry the onion and garlic in the oil until they're soft, then add them to the lentils and season the mixture with sea salt and freshly ground black pepper to taste.

To make the tomato filling, fry the onion and garlic in the oil (I usually do this with the onion and garlic for the lentil mixture, then take out half to mix with the lentils, leaving the rest in the saucepan), then add the tomatoes and boil fairly rapidly for about 10 minutes, until most of the liquid has evaporated and the mixture is thick. Add the oregano and season with sea salt and freshly ground black pepper.

Next prepare the spinach filling. Wash the spinach thoroughly in three changes of cold water, then cook it in a dry saucepan over a fairly high heat, with a lid on the saucepan, until it's tender – 7-10 minutes. Chop the spinach in the saucepan using the end of a fish slice, then drain off all the liquid and add the butter, plenty of sea salt and freshly ground black pepper and some grated nutmeg.

Now, to assemble and finish the 'gâteau'. First of all set the oven to 350°F (180°C), mark 4. Put one of the pancakes on a flat ovenproof plate and spread it with a third of the lentil mixture. Place another pancake on top and cover with a third of the tomato sauce, then lay another pancake on that, followed by a third of the spinach. Continue in layers in this way until all the pancakes have been used. Pour the sauce over the top of the 'gâteau'; sprinkle with grated cheese. Put it into the oven for about 40 minutes to heat through. Garnish with the tomato slices and parsley. It's nice served with a contrasting vegetable such as buttered carrots.

PANCAKES WITH LENTIL AND MUSHROOM FILLING

As in the lentil and tomato soup recipe, it seems to be all right to cook the lentils with the tomatoes because they're quick-cooking and there's also some stock to take off some of the acidity which can prevent pulses from softening properly.

For the pancakes:
basic pancake batter (see page 162)
oil for frying

For the filling:
1 large onion, peeled and chopped
2 cloves garlic, crushed
1 oz (25 g) butter
2 tablespoons oil
6 oz (175 g) split red lentils
½ pint (275 ml) water *or* un-salted stock
14 oz (397 g) can tomatoes
½ teaspoon ground cumin
2 tablespoons red wine
8 oz (225 g) button mushrooms, wiped and sliced
sea salt
freshly ground black pepper

To finish:
¾ pint (400 ml) well-flavoured white sauce
2 oz (50 g) grated cheese

SERVES 4-6

Using the basic pancake batter, make 10-12 thin pancakes, then leave them on one side to cool while you make the filling.

Fry the onion and garlic in the butter and oil in a medium-sized saucepan for 5 minutes, then stir in the lentils, water or stock, tomatoes, cumin and wine, and let the mixture simmer gently, uncovered, for 30 minutes. Add the mushrooms and cook for a further 5-6 minutes, then season with sea salt and freshly ground black pepper. Preheat oven to 350°F (180°C), mark 4.

Spread a little of the lentil mixture on each pancake; roll the pancakes up neatly and arrange them side by side in a well-greased, shallow ovenproof dish. Pour the sauce over the pancake rolls, sprinkle with grated cheese and bake in the oven for 30-40 minutes.

PANCAKES WITH SPINACH AND CONTINENTAL LENTIL FILLING

This dish, featuring those excellent partners, continental lentils and spinach, is very tasty and filling. It's nice with a fresh tomato salad.

For the pancakes:
basic pancake batter (see page 162)
oil for frying

For the lentil filling:
4 oz (125 g) continental lentils, soaked overnight in cold water
2 tablespoons oil
1 oz (25 g) butter
1 onion, peeled and chopped
1 clove garlic, crushed
6 oz (175 g) mushrooms, wiped and sliced
1 tablespoon tomato purée
sea salt
freshly ground black pepper

For the spinach filling:
1 lb (450 g) spinach
½ oz (13 g) butter
grated nutmeg

To finish:
¾ pint (400 ml) cheese sauce
3 oz (75 g) grated cheese

SERVES 4-6

First of all make 10 or 12 thin pancakes. Then make the fillings. Drain and rinse the lentils, put them into a saucepan with cold water to cover and simmer for about 40 minutes, until they're tender. Meanwhile heat the oil and butter in another saucepan and fry the onion and garlic for 5 minutes, then add the mushrooms and cook for another 5 minutes. Drain the lentils and add them to the onion and mushroom mixture, together with the tomato purée and some sea salt and freshly ground black pepper.

For the spinach filling, wash the spinach thoroughly in three changes of water, then cook it as usual in a dry saucepan over rather a high heat for about 7-10 minutes, until it's tender. Drain and chop the spinach, then add the butter and a good seasoning of sea salt, freshly ground black pepper and nutmeg.

Preheat the oven to 350°F (180°C), mark 4. Put a rounded tablespoon of lentil mixture on the centre of a pancake and roll the pancake round it; repeat until you've used up all the lentil mixture and half the pancakes, then fill the remaining pancakes with spinach in the same way. Arrange the pancakes in a well-greased, shallow ovenproof dish, alternating the two types, then pour the cheese sauce evenly over them, sprinkle with grated cheese, and bake for 30-40 minutes, until piping hot and golden brown on top.

INDIAN RICE PANCAKES WITH SPLIT PEA FILLING

These Indian pancakes are different from the others in this section because the batter is made from a mixture of rice, milk and split peas and contains no eggs. This gives a delicious, rather 'nutty' flavour, and a slightly different texture. I find it best to make the pancakes fairly small – certainly using no more than 2 tablespoons of batter per pancake – as they are then more manageable.

A liquidizer is essential for this recipe (unless you want to spend hours grinding up the rice and peas in true Indian style), and you need to start preparations the day before you want to make it. I've tried the pancakes without the fermentation period and they don't work as well, so it's best to be patient.

8 oz (225 g) long grain brown rice
8 oz (225 g) yellow split peas
1 teaspoon sea salt
½ pint (275 ml) water
½ pint (275 ml) milk and water mixed
1 onion, peeled and chopped

1 clove garlic, crushed
2 tablespoons vegetable oil
1 teaspoon ground cumin
1 teaspoon ground turmeric
2 teaspoons lemon juice
freshly ground black pepper
oil for shallow frying

SERVES 4

Put the brown rice and split peas into separate bowls, cover them well with cold water and leave to soak overnight. Next day, rinse them and remove one third of the split peas; cover these with cold water and cook them until they're tender, then leave them on one side for the pancake filling. Put the remaining split peas and all the rice into the liquidizer goblet, together with the ½ pint (275 ml) water and a teaspoonful of sea salt and whizz them together to a smooth, creamy purée. Turn the purée into a bowl and leave in a warm place for 12 hours, or overnight, to ferment. Next day add the milk and water to the purée and whip it until smooth and creamy.

To make the pancakes, heat a little oil in a frying pan and pour in 1-2 tablespoonfuls of the batter. I find these pancakes take a little longer to cook than the ordinary type, and if you try to turn them over too soon they will collapse. So let the pancake cook thoroughly underneath and test it by lifting the edge with a palette knife. If it feels firm and looks brown, carefully turn it over and cook the other side.

I usually serve these crispy pancakes flat, with the filling simply spooned on top, but they can be rolled round the filling and placed side by side in a shallow dish if you prefer. They are not difficult to do once you get used to the texture.

To make the filling, fry the onion and garlic in the oil with the spices for about 10 minutes, without browning, then stir in the reserved, cooked split peas and heat through. Add lemon juice to taste and season with sea salt and freshly ground black pepper.

The mixture of rice and split peas is of course excellent from the nutritional point of view because it brings together two complementary proteins.

CHICK PEAS WITH PASTA – *TUONI E LAMPO*

The Italian name for this dish means 'thunder and lightning' and refers to the texture of the two main ingredients, the soft pasta and the firm chick peas! It is surprisingly tasty, but you really do need to use olive oil to give the right flavour. Traditionally it is made with different shapes of white pasta but I generally use one of the wholewheat ones because I think they're healthier.

8 oz (225 g) chick peas	sea salt
8 oz (225 g) thin wholewheat macaroni	freshly ground black pepper
4 tablespoons olive oil	*To serve:*
1 large clove garlic, crushed	plenty of dry, grated cheese

SERVES 4

Soak the chick peas for several hours in plenty of cold water,

172

then drain and rinse them, put them into a saucepan with a good covering of fresh, cold water and simmer them gently until they're tender. Drain the chick peas and keep them warm. Cook the wholewheat macaroni in boiling, salted water, until it's just tender, then drain it. Heat the olive oil in a large saucepan and add the garlic, chick peas and pasta, together with sea salt and freshly ground black pepper to taste, and toss them gently together until everything is glossy with the oil. Serve immediately with a good sprinkling of cheese and a tossed green salad.

SPAGHETTI WITH CONTINENTAL LENTIL SAUCE

Pulses make lovely sauces for spaghetti, and the use of a pressure cooker can put this kind of dish into the 'quick meal' class. It's very nourishing and satisfying, too.

6 oz (175 g) continental lentils
1 onion
2 cloves garlic
2 tablespoons oil
4 oz (125 g) mushrooms, wiped and sliced
1 small green pepper, de-seeded and chopped
2 tomatoes, peeled and chopped
1 tablespoon red wine
1 tablespoon tomato purée
1 teaspoon ground coriander
pinch of chilli powder
sea salt
freshly ground black pepper
8 oz (225 g) wholewheat or buckwheat spaghetti
½ oz (13 g) butter

To serve:
grated cheese

SERVES 4

If there's time to get organized in advance, soak the lentils in
cold water for a few hours, then drain and rinse them. If
you're in a hurry, just wash the lentils. Put them into a saucepan, cover with cold water and simmer gently until they're
tender – about 40 minutes if they've been soaked, 1-1¼ hours if
not, or around 15 minutes in a pressure cooker.

Meanwhile peel and chop the onion and crush the garlic.
Fry them together in the oil for 5 minutes, then add the mushrooms and green pepper and cook for a further 5 minutes or so.
Drain the lentils and stir them into the vegetable mixture,
together with the tomatoes, wine, purée and seasonings. Let
the mixture simmer gently while you cook the spaghetti in
plenty of boiling, salted water. Drain it when it's just tender,
put it back into the hot saucepan and add the butter, turning
the spaghetti until the butter has melted and the spaghetti
looks all glossy and appetizing. Then turn the spaghetti on to a
warm serving dish, pour the lentil sauce on top of it and sprinkle
with grated cheese. This is lovely with a crisp green salad.

SPAGHETTI WITH LENTIL AND TOMATO SAUCE

As split red lentils cook in under half an hour without soaking,
this dish is useful for those times when you suddenly find your-
self having to produce a meal quickly, particularly as the
ingredients are basic store-cupboard ones. The protein content
of this recipe is excellent, because the pulse and wholewheat
complement each other.

2 tablespoons oil
1 large onion, peeled and chopped
1 large clove garlic, crushed
14 oz (397 g) can tomatoes
½ teaspoon dried basil *or* oregano
½ teaspoon powdered cinnamon
8 oz (225 g) split red lentils, washed
¾ pint (400 ml) water

2 tablespoons red wine (if possible)
sea salt
freshly ground black pepper

For spaghetti:
8 oz (225 g) wholewheat or buckwheat spaghetti
½ oz (13 g) butter

To serve:
a little grated cheese

SERVES 4

Heat the oil in a largish saucepan and fry the onion and garlic until they're tender – about 10 minutes; then add the tomatoes, herbs, cinnamon, lentils, water and wine and bring up to the boil. Simmer mixture with a lid on the saucepan for about 25 minutes, until the lentils are tender. Taste, and season with sea salt and freshly ground black pepper.

About 10 minutes before the lentils are done, start cooking the spaghetti. Half-fill a large saucepan with water, add some sea salt and bring to the boil. Add the spaghetti to the saucepan by holding it upright in the boiling water and gradually pushing it down into the water as it softens. Simmer the spaghetti until it's just tender, or 'al dente', as the Italians say, then drain it and add the butter and a good grinding of black pepper. Pile the spaghetti on to a warm serving dish, pour the sauce on top and sprinkle with grated cheese. Serve with a nice crisp green salad.

PASTICHIO

I must admit that this is really rather a corruption of a Greek dish, but the original is so good I wanted to make a vegetarian one with pulses. Strictly speaking, pastichio should be made with a layer of pasta, a layer of spicy beef mince mixture, a thick cream sauce and a thin cream sauce. My version consists of the pasta and spicy lentils topped with a creamy sauce. It's very filling and people seem to enjoy it.

8 oz (225 g) split red lentils
2 oz (50 g) butter
1 large onion, peeled and chopped
2-3 cloves garlic, crushed
1 small green pepper, deseeded and chopped
4 oz (125 g) mushrooms, sliced
14 oz (397 g) can tomatoes
½ teaspoon dried oregano
½ teaspoon cinnamon
½ glass red wine

¾ pint (400 ml) water *or* unsalted stock
sea salt
freshly ground black pepper
6 oz (175 g) wholewheat macaroni

For the topping:
2 eggs
¾ pint (400 ml) well-flavoured white sauce
3 oz (75 g) grated cheese

SERVES 6

Wash and pick over the lentils. Melt the butter in a large saucepan and fry the onion for 5 minutes, until it's beginning to soften, then add the garlic, green pepper and mushrooms and cook for a further 5 minutes or so, stirring from time to time. Mix in the tomatoes, the washed lentils, the oregano and cinnamon, wine and water or stock. Bring up to the boil, give it a good stir, then leave it to simmer gently for about 45 minutes, until the lentils are soft and the liquid has boiled away to leave a lovely thick, rich mixture. Season carefully with sea salt and freshly ground black pepper and add a little more cinnamon and oregano if you think it can take it – the mixture should be quite highly seasoned.

When the lentils are nearly done, set the oven to 400°F (200°C), mark 6, then cook the macaroni by plunging it into a saucepan of fast-boiling salted water and boiling until it's just tender; drain it and put it into a well-buttered, shallow oblong ovenproof dish. Spoon the lentil mixture on top. Beat the eggs into the white sauce, then pour that evenly over the lentils and sprinkle with the grated cheese. Bake the pastichio in the centre of the oven for 40-50 minutes, until it's piping hot with a lovely golden brown top. Serve with a herby green salad.

LENTIL LASAGNE

This is a lovely tasty dish, packed with protein. Serve it with buttery French beans or broccoli and I'm sure no one will miss their meat.

12 oz (350 g) continental lentils
1 large onion, peeled and chopped
2 cloves garlic, crushed
1 oz (25 g) butter
2 tablespoons oil
1 pint (550 ml) water *or* un-salted stock
1 teaspoon ground coriander

sea salt
freshly ground black pepper
8 oz (225 g) wholewheat lasagne

For topping:
2 eggs
1 pint (550 ml) well-flavoured white sauce
4 oz (125 g) grated cheese

SERVES 6-8

Wash and pick over the lentils, then cover them with cold water and leave them to soak for several hours. Fry the onion and garlic in the butter and oil in a medium-sized saucepan for 10 minutes, then add the lentils and stir for a minute or two so that the lentils are coated with the garlic and fat. Mix in the water, bring up to the boil and simmer gently, uncovered, for about 45 minutes, when the lentils should be tender and the mixture thick. Mix in the coriander and season with sea salt and freshly ground black pepper.

Set the oven for 400°F (200°C), mark 6. Cook the lasagne in boiling, salted water until it's tender, then drain it well. Beat the eggs into the white sauce.

Put half the lentil mixture into the base of a well-greased shallow ovenproof casserole dish and arrange half the lasagne slices on top, then pour in half the sauce mixture. Repeat the layers, ending with the sauce, and sprinkle the top with grated cheese. Bake in the centre of the oven for 40-50 minutes, until it's all bubbling and golden brown.

SPAGHETTI AND BEAN BAKE

Tasty, filling and full of protein, this really only needs a green salad to go with it.

6 oz (175 g) haricot or butter beans

2 large onions, peeled and chopped

2 large cloves garlic, crushed

4 tablespoons olive oil

4 oz (125 g) mushrooms, washed and chopped

2 14 oz (397 g) cans tomatoes

3 tablespoons tomato purée

2 tablespoons red wine if available

1 teaspoon oregano *or* basil
1 teaspoon cinnamon
2-3 tablespoons chopped parsley
½ teaspoon chilli powder
sea salt
freshly ground black pepper
sugar

6 oz (175 g) thin wholewheat or buckwheat spaghetti

To finish:
dry crumbs
a little grated cheese
a little butter

SERVES 6

Soak, rinse and cook the beans, then drain them. Next, make a tomato sauce: fry the onion and garlic in the olive oil in a largish saucepan for 10 minutes, then stir in the mushrooms and cook for a further 4-5 minutes. Add the tomatoes, tomato purée, the red wine if you're using it, and the oregano or basil, cinnamon, parsley and chilli powder. Let the sauce simmer, without a lid on the saucepan, for 10 minutes or so, until the vegetables are all cooked and the liquid has reduced to a thickish purée. Season with sea salt, freshly ground black pepper and a little sugar to taste.

Preheat the oven to 350°F (180°C), mark 4. Cook the spaghetti in plenty of boiling salted water until it's just tender, then drain it well. Grease a 3 pint (1.7 l) shallow ovenproof casserole and spread a layer of half the spaghetti in the base; arrange half the beans on top and pour in half the sauce. Repeat the layers, ending with a layer of sauce and sprinkle generously with dry crumbs and grated cheese; dot with butter. Bake in the oven for 45-50 minutes, until golden and crisp on top.

Pastry Dishes

As with pulses and rice and pulses and pasta, putting pulses with pastry immediately brings together two complementary proteins, ending up with first-class protein and a very satisfying, filling meal. A shade too filling, perhaps, for weight-watchers, but splendid food for hungry families, and those counting calories can always have a smaller portion of the pastry with plenty of salad or green vegetables instead of potatoes.

If the pulses and pastry are going to be really delicious together, they've both got to be light. Solid lentils in heavy pastry would be dreary beyond belief. But a flan of tender beans, mushrooms and onions in a light, well-flavoured custard on a crisp pastry base, or well-cooked butter beans with leeks and tomatoes, topped with golden puff pastry are another thing altogether and always seem to go down well.

There are three basic pastry recipes which I find useful with pulses. Two of these use 100 per cent wholewheat flour, which I really prefer from the health point of view, and the other, a quick puff pastry, uses 81 per cent wholewheat, which is not quite so nutritious, but useful for occasions when you want a really light result. I'm giving the recipes for these three pastries at the beginning of this section, so that they're all together, and to save repetition in the recipes. All of keep them well, the puff pastry, ready made, wrapped in polythene in the freezer, the other two in their 'rubbed in' stage, in a container in the refrigerator, ready just to have water added when you want to use them anything up to six weeks later.

PUFF PASTRY

8 oz (225 g) hard margarine *or* butter
¼ pint (150 ml) ice-cold water

tiny squeeze of lemon juice
8 oz (225 g) plain 81 per cent flour

Make sure the butter or margarine is really hard and the water as cold as possible: I usually put both in the refrigerator for a few hours before making the pastry. It's a good idea to put the plain flour into a large bowl and chill that, too, if you can; one of the secrets of success with this pastry is to have everything, including your hands, as cold as possible.

Cut the butter into ¼ inch (6 mm) dice and put them into the bowl with the plain flour. Mix lightly so that the butter gets dusted with plain flour, then add the water and lemon juice and mix gently with a metal spoon to make a loose, lumpy dough.

Put the dough on to a lightly floured board and turn it once or twice in a little plain flour, then roll it out into a long oblong, using short, firm strokes. Fold the top third of the oblong down and the bottom third up so that you have three layers. Half-turn the slab of pastry to the right, so that the folded edges are at the sides. Roll, fold and turn the pastry again, doing this four times in all. Put the fold of dough into a poly-thene bag and chill it in the coldest part of the refrigerator for at least two hours before using it. To use the dough, roll it out to the required shape on a lightly floured board.

WHOLEWHEAT SHORTCRUST PASTRY (FOR FLANS)

Flan pastry should be crisp, thin and light. To achieve this result with 100 per cent wholewheat flour I find it best to use plain flour and butter or a mixture of butter and margarine. If you mix the 100 per cent flour with a proportion of 81 per cent – two thirds 100 per cent to one third 81 per cent, or half and half – the pastry is even lighter and crisper.

8 oz (225 g) plain 100 per cent wholewheat flour
pinch of sea salt
2 oz (50 g) vegetable marga-rine
2 oz (50 g) butter
2 tablespoons cold water

Sift the wholewheat flour and sea salt into a bowl; there will be a small residue of bran left in the sieve, add this too. Cut the fats into pieces, then, using your fingertips, rub the fats into the wholewheat flour until the mixture resembles fine breadcrumbs. Add the water and gently gather the pastry together into a ball; turn it on to a floured board and knead very lightly. Then roll it out and use as required.

WHOLEWHEAT SHORTCRUST PASTRY (FOR PIES)

I like a wholewheat pie crust to be light and crumbly, and to achieve this result I find it best to use a self-raising 100 per cent flour with a mixture of half margarine and half vegetable shortening.

8 oz (225 g) self-raising 100 per cent wholewheat flour *or* use plain with 2 teaspoons of baking powder

pinch of sea salt

2 oz (50 g) vegetable margarine

2 oz (50 g) vegetable shortening

2 tablespoons cold water

Sift the wholewheat flour (with baking powder, if you're using it) and sea salt into a bowl; mix in the residue of bran which will be left in the sieve. Cut the fats into pieces, add them to the bowl, then rub them into the flour using your fingertips, until the mixture resembles fine wholewheat breadcrumbs. Then gradually add the cold water to make a dough. Turn the pastry on to a floured board, knead lightly and use as required.

BUTTER BEAN AND LEEK PIE

This makes a lovely family meal; serve it with a cooked green vegetable and potatoes, too, if you're catering for a hungry, growing family.

4 oz (125 g) butter beans

2 oz (50 g) margarine

8 oz (225 g) carrots, scraped and diced small

1 lb (450 g) leeks, cleaned and cut into ½ inch (1 cm) slices

4 oz (125 g) mushrooms, wiped and sliced

1 tablespoon flour

8 oz (225 g) canned tomatoes

¼ pint (150 ml) stock

sea salt

freshly ground black pepper

For pie crust:

8 oz (225 g) puff pastry (half the quantity given in the basic recipe on page 181)

a little beaten egg to glaze, if required

SERVES 4

Soak, drain and rinse the butter beans, then cook them until

183

they're tender and drain well.

Preheat the oven to 425°F (220°C), mark 7. Melt the margarine in a medium-sized saucepan, then put in the carrots, cover and cook very gently without browning for 10 minutes; add the leeks and mushrooms and cook for a further 10 minutes. Sprinkle the flour over the vegetables, then stir so that it gets mixed with the fat. Mix in the tomatoes and stock and cook gently, stirring, for 2-3 minutes, until thickened. Add the butter beans to the saucepan and season with sea salt and freshly ground black pepper. Turn the mixture into a 2 pint (1 l) pie dish; cool.

Roll out the pastry on a lightly floured board and use it to cover the top of the pie. Crimp the edges and decorate the top of the pie with little pastry cut-outs if you're feeling that way inclined. Brush the surface of the pastry with beaten egg if you want a shiny finish. Bake in preheated oven for 20 minutes, then reduce heat to 375°F (190°C), mark 5 for a further 15 minutes.

BUTTER BEAN AND TOMATO PIE

The wholewheat crust gives this pie a lovely country look, but it's also good made with the puff pastry, like the butter bean and leek pie.

6 oz (175 g) butter beans
1 large onion
2 oz (50 g) margarine
1 tablespoon tomato purée
14 oz (397 g) can tomatoes
½ teaspoon dried basil
sea salt
freshly ground black pepper

a little sugar

For the pie crust:
6 oz (175 g) wholewheat shortcrust pastry (page 182)
beaten egg to glaze, if liked

SERVES 4

Soak the butter beans for several hours, then drain and rinse them, cover with cold water and cook until tender, then drain.

Preheat the oven to 425°F (220°C), mark 7. Peel and chop the onion and fry it in the margarine for 10 minutes, then add the tomato purée, tomatoes, basil and a seasoning of sea salt, freshly ground black pepper and a dash of sugar (if you think it needs it), and simmer gently for 10 minutes. Mix in the butter beans, check seasoning and pour into a 2 pint (1 l) pie dish.

Roll out the pastry and use it to cover the top of the pie. Crimp the edges and decorate the top as required. Bake the pie in the preheated oven for 20 minutes, then turn the heat down to 375°F (190°C), mark 5 and cook for a further 10-15 minutes.

LENTIL AND TOMATO PIE

1 large onion

2 oz (50 g) butter *or* margarine

1 large clove garlic, crushed

6 oz (175 g) split red lentils, washed

12 fl oz (350 ml) unsalted stock *or* water

2 tomatoes, skinned and chopped

3 oz (75 g) grated cheese

1 teaspoon dried basil

1 tablespoon lemon juice

1 egg

sea salt

freshly ground black pepper

For the crust:

8 oz (225 g) shortcrust pastry (page 182)

To glaze:

beaten egg

SERVES 4-6

First make the filling: peel and chop the onion and fry it in the

185

butter or margarine in a good-sized saucepan until it's golden and beginning to soften, about 5-6 minutes, then add the split red lentils and garlic and stir for a moment or two before adding the stock or water. Bring the mixture up to the boil, half-cover with a lid and simmer for about 20 minutes, until the lentils are soft and pale golden. Remove the saucepan from the heat and add the tomatoes, cheese, basil, lemon juice, egg and sea salt and freshly ground black pepper to taste. Leave the mixture to cool.

Roll out about two-thirds of the pastry and use to line an 8 inch (20 cm) flan dish or sandwich tin. Roll the remainder into a circle to fit the top of the dish.

Preheat the oven to 400°F (200°C), mark 6. Spread the lentil mixture into the pastry case. Dampen the edges of the pastry with a little cold water, then put the circle of pastry on top and press down lightly, crimping the edges. Prick the top and brush with a little beaten egg if you want a shiny finish. Bake the pie in the preheated oven for about 40 minutes, until the pastry is golden brown and crisp.

BUTTER BEAN AND ONION FLAN

This is a lovely tasty flan, packed with protein.

6 oz (175 g) wholewheat shortcrust pastry (page 182)

For the filling:
1 large onion
1 oz (25 g) butter
4 oz (125 g) grated cheese
1 teaspoon dry mustard

1 egg
¼ pint (150 ml) milk
sea salt
freshly ground black pepper
4 oz (125 g) butter beans, soaked, cooked and then drained
1 tablespoon chopped parsley

SERVES 4-6

Preheat oven to 425°F (220°C), mark 7. Roll out the pastry and use it to line an 8 inch (20 cm) flan dish. Prick the base of the flan, then bake it in the oven for about 15 minutes, until firm and crisp. Turn oven heat down to 350°F (180°C), mark 4.

Peel and slice the onion and fry it in the butter for about 10 minutes, until it's soft but not browned. Mix together the cheese and mustard; beat the egg with the milk and season with sea salt and freshly ground black pepper. Put the hot cooked onion straight into the hot flan case and arrange the butter beans on top. Sprinkle with the cheese and mustard mixture, then pour in the egg and milk and scatter with the chopped parsley. Bake for 40-50 minutes, until set and golden brown. I think it's nicest served hot or warm, but you can also serve it cold. You can freeze it, too, but the pastry is never as crisp afterwards, I find.

CHICK PEA AND MUSHROOM FLAN

I think this flan is best served hot, with a crisp salad or cooked green vegetable.

6 oz (175 g) shortcrust pastry (page 182)

For the filling:
1 oz (25 g) butter
1 onion, peeled and sliced
1 large clove garlic, crushed
4 oz (125 g) button mushrooms, wiped and sliced

4 oz (125 g) chick peas, soaked, cooked and drained
1 tablespoon chopped parsley
sea salt
freshly ground black pepper
1 egg
¼ pint top of the milk
3 oz (75 g) grated cheese

SERVES 6

Preheat the oven to 425°F (220°C), mark 7. Roll out the pastry and line an 8 inch (20 cm) flan dish; prick the base and bake in the oven for 15 minutes.

Make the filling by melting the butter in a saucepan and frying the onion and garlic for about 10 minutes, until tender but not browned; then add the mushrooms and cook for a further 3-4 minutes. Stir in the cooked chick peas and the chopped parsley and season with sea salt and freshly ground black pepper. Put the mixture straight into the hot flan case. Beat together the egg and top of the milk, season with sea salt and freshly ground black pepper, and pour into the flan case; scatter the grated cheese over the top. Bake the flan in the preheated oven for 40-50 minutes until it's set and golden brown. As with the other flans, different beans can be used according to your inclination and store-cupboard.

HARICOT, PEPPER AND TOMATO FLAN

This is another tasty mixture. It's lovely with a bowl of crisp, mixed salad or with cooked green beans or buttery young carrots.

6 oz (175 g) shortcrust pastry (page 182)

For the filling:
1 oz (25 g) butter
1 onion, peeled and sliced
1 clove garlic, crushed
1 medium-sized green pepper, de-seeded and sliced

2 tomatoes, skinned and sliced
½ teaspoon dried basil
4 oz (125 g) haricot beans, soaked, cooked and drained
sea salt
freshly ground black pepper
1 egg
¼ pint (150 ml) top of the milk

SERVES 6

Preheat oven to 425°F (220°C), mark 7. Roll out the pastry and line an 8 inch (20 cm) flan dish. Prick the base and bake the flan in the oven for about 15 minutes, until crisp. Reduce heat to 350°F (180°C), mark 4.

Meanwhile make the filling. Melt the butter in a medium-sized saucepan and fry the onion, garlic and green pepper for 10 minutes. Remove from the heat and add the tomatoes, basil and haricot beans. Season with sea salt and freshly ground black pepper and pour this mixture into the hot flan case.

Beat together the egg and the top of the milk, season it with sea salt and freshly ground black pepper and then pour it carefully into the flan case. Bake for 40-50 minutes, until set and golden. Serve hot or cold.

Of course other types of beans can also be used for this flan. Cannellini beans, butter beans, flageolet beans and red kidney beans are all suitable.

LENTIL AND GREEN PEPPER FLAN

Apart from its pleasant flavour, the green pepper looks attractive in this flan because it contrasts well with the colour of the lentils.

6 oz (175 g) shortcrust pastry (page 182)

For the filling:
6 oz (175 g) split red lentils
12 fl oz (350 ml) water *or* unsalted stock
1 onion, peeled and chopped

1 clove garlic, crushed
1 oz (25 g) butter
1 green pepper
4 oz (125 g) grated cheese
1 tablespoon tomato purée
1 egg
sea salt
freshly ground black pepper

SERVES 6

Set the oven to 425°F (220°C), mark 7. Roll out the pastry and line an 8 inch (20 cm) flan dish; prick the base and bake in the oven for 15 minutes, or until set and golden brown. Take it out of the oven and set on one side. Turn the oven down to 350°F (180°C), mark 4.

Wash and pick over the lentils, then put them into a saucepan with the water or stock and simmer gently until tender – 20-30 minutes. Fry the onion and garlic in the butter, without browning, for about 5 minutes. While that's happening, wash the green pepper and slice it into thin rings, discarding the seeds. Add it to the onions and garlic in the saucepan and cook for about 5 minutes, then add the onion and pepper mixture to the cooked lentils, together with the grated cheese, tomato purée, egg and sea salt and freshly ground black pepper to taste. Spread the mixture into the prepared flan case and bake in the oven for about 40 minutes.

LENTIL, TOMATO AND MUSHROOM FLAN

This flan is nice hot or cold; if we're having it hot I sometimes serve a parsley sauce which seems to go well with it.

6 oz (175 g) shortcrust pastry (page 182)

For the filling:
6 oz (175 g) split red lentils
12 fl oz (350 ml) unsalted stock *or* water
1 large onion, peeled and chopped

1 oz (25 g) butter
4 oz (125 g) mushrooms, wiped and sliced
1 tablespoon chopped parsley
4 oz (125 g) grated cheese
1 egg
sea salt
freshly ground black pepper
2 tomatoes

SERVES 6

Preheat the oven to 425°F (220°C), mark 7. Use the pastry to line an 8 inch (20 cm) flan dish, prick the base and bake the flan in the oven for about 15 minutes, until it's set and crisp. Turn the oven down to 350°F (180°C), mark 4.

Wash and pick over the lentils, then put them into a saucepan with the stock or water and cook until they're tender and have absorbed all the water – 20-30 minutes.

Fry the onion in the butter in a medium-sized saucepan for 10 minutes, but don't brown it, then add the mushrooms and cook for another 3-4 minutes. Stir in the cooked lentils, parsley, grated cheese, egg and plenty of seasoning. Spoon the mixture into the cooked flan case and smooth the top. Slice the tomatoes and arrange them on the top of the flan. Bake in the oven for about 40 minutes – watch it towards the end so that it doesn't get too dry.

RED BEAN AND TOMATO FLAN

The red beans, tomatoes and parsley make this a colourful flan. I think it's nice made with soured cream, but you could use single cream or top-of-the-milk.

6 oz (175 g) shortcrust pastry (page 182)

For the filling:
1 onion, peeled and chopped
1 clove garlic, crushed
2 tablespoons oil
3 tomatoes, skinned and chopped

4 oz (125 g) red kidney beans, soaked, cooked and drained
¼ pint (150 ml) soured cream
1 egg
½ teaspoon paprika pepper
pinch chilli powder
sea salt
freshly ground black pepper
1 tablespoon chopped parsley

SERVES 6

Preheat the oven to 425°F (220°C), mark 7. Use the pastry to line an 8 inch (20 cm) flan dish. Prick the base of the flan and bake in the oven for 15 minutes. Remove the flan from the oven; turn the heat down to 350°F (180°C), mark 4.

Next, make the filling. Fry the onion and garlic in the oil in a medium-sized saucepan for 10 minutes. Remove the saucepan from the heat and add the tomatoes and beans. You can mash the beans a little as you mix them in, or leave them whole, whichever you prefer. In a small bowl, beat together the soured cream and the egg, then stir them into the bean mixture, together with the paprika, a good pinch of chilli powder and sea salt and freshly ground black pepper to taste. Pour the mixture into the flan case and sprinkle with the chopped parsley. Bake the flan in the oven for 35-40 minutes, until it's set.

This flan is lovely warm, with a green salad.

MUSHROOM, TOMATO AND HARICOT VOL AU VENTS

You can use bought puff pastry for these, or the puff pastry given at the beginning of this section. The little vol au vents are tasty and full of protein.

puff pastry (page 181)
a little beaten egg to glaze

For the filling:
1 large onion, peeled and chopped

2 cloves garlic, crushed
1 oz (25 g) butter
8 oz (225 g) button mushrooms, wiped and sliced
8 oz (225 g) canned tomatoes
a little cold water or stock

1 rounded tablespoon flour

4 tablespoons double cream

4 oz (125 g) haricot beans, cooked and drained

1 tablespoon chopped parsley

sea salt

freshly ground black pepper

SERVES 4-6

Set oven to 425°F (220°C), mark 7. Roll the pastry out ½ inch (1 cm) thick and, using a 2½ inch (5 cm) round cutter, cut out 12 circles. Sprinkle a little cold water on a baking sheet and place the puff pastry circles on it. With a 1½ inch (3.5 cm) round cutter make another cut on each circle, but don't go right through. Brush the vol au vents with beaten egg and bake them in the oven for 15-20 minutes, until they're risen and golden. Remove from the oven and place them on a cooling tray. Using a sharp knife, carefully remove the central 'lid' of each and scoop out any excess pastry to make room for the filling.

While the vol au vent cases are cooking, make the filling. Fry the onion and garlic gently in the oil in a large saucepan for 10 minutes, then add the mushrooms and cook for a further 4-5 minutes. Drain the tomatoes; measure the liquid and make it up to ½ pint (275 ml) with some cold water or stock. Add the tomatoes and liquid to the mushrooms and onion in the saucepan and simmer for 15 minutes, without a lid on the saucepan. Blend the flour smoothly with the cream and add to the onion mixture, together with the beans, parsley and sea salt and freshly ground black pepper to taste. Cook gently for 10 minutes, stirring often. Check seasoning.

Spoon the bean mixture into the vol au vent cases and put the lids on top. Serve warm.

With Rice and Cereals

The Hindus have a saying: 'Rice is good, but lentils are my life', but I would add that if you put the two together you have the most potent combination of all. Actually this mixture of pulses and rice happens naturally in dishes all over the world, from the dals and rice of India to the red beans and rice of the West Indies and the red rice of Japan. Certainly the two foods taste good together, and their proteins complement each other, offering excellent nourishment.

I've used brown rice in all the recipes because I like its flavour and also because it's more nutritious than white rice. Short grain brown rice is only used in one recipe, the Japanese red rice; for everything else I use the long grain variety. I find quite a variation in the types of long grain brown rice available; my favourite is the one with the most slender, pointed grains and I find that this cooks up beautifully, nutty in flavour, firm in texture, every grain separate.

Cooking brown rice is easy when you know how, but it does take longer than white rice. First of all, it needs careful washing, and sometimes careful picking over, too, to remove small pieces of grit and stone which may have crept in, especially if the rice was bought loose. When it's clean, put the rice into a saucepan – one with a heavy base and tight-fitting lid is best – and cover it with 1¾ times its volume in cold water. That is, if you've one cup of rice, you'll need 1¾ cups of water, but as recipes usually give quantities by weight, it's handy to know that for 8 oz (225 g) brown rice this is in fact ¾ pint (400 ml) water. Add a little sea salt and put the saucepan over a high heat until the water boils, then give the rice a stir, put the lid on the saucepan and turn the heat right down. Leave the rice to cook very gently for 45 minutes. Then when you lift the lid, you should see a pan of lovely fluffy rice, tender and dry with no water in the saucepan. If there is still a little water and the rice is not quite cooked, take the saucepan off the heat, put the lid back on, and just leave the rice to steam in its own heat for another 10-15 minutes, after which all should be well.

Recently I've discovered another way of cooking rice which involves soaking and then steaming it. You have to allow several hours for the rice to soak, but after that the actual cooking takes only about 30 minutes, so rice left to soak during the day can be more speedily cooked for an evening meal. Wash and pick over the rice as usual, put it into a bowl with a good covering of cold water and leave it for 4-5 hours (or, preferably, overnight). Then drain the rice, place it in the top of a steamer and steam for about 30 minutes until the grains are tender. Stir in a little sea salt to taste when the rice is cooked. I find the rice cooks beautifully and I use this method a lot for plain boiled rice to serve with other dishes.

Like the pasta and pancake dishes, rice and pulse dishes need little in the way of accompaniments and so are easy-going on the cook. Mango chutney or lime pickle are nice with some of the curried recipes, and so are Indian breads, chapatis and puris, recipes for which I'm giving at the beginning of this section, together with one for spicy fried rice, which is useful for serving with a number of the pulse dishes.

FRIED RICE

8 oz (225 g) long grain brown rice

2 tablespoons ghee *or* vegetable oil

¾ pint (400 ml) boiling water

1 teaspoon turmeric

3 cloves

2 inch (5 cm) cinnamon stick

2 or 3 cardamom pods

1 bayleaf

sea salt

freshly ground black pepper

SERVES 4

Wash the rice thoroughly, then drain it and, if possible, leave it for half an hour or so to dry. Heat the ghee or oil in a heavy-based saucepan and add the drained rice. Fry over a gentle heat, stirring continuously, until the rice has become opaque, but do not let it brown – takes about 5 minutes. Then add the boiling water, turmeric, cloves, cinnamon, cardamom pods, bayleaf and a seasoning of sea salt and freshly ground black pepper. When the mixture is boiling vigorously, turn the heat down and put a lid on the saucepan. Leave it to cook very gently for 45 minutes, after which the rice should be tender and the liquid absorbed. Remove cloves, cinnamon stick, cardamom pods and the bayleaf.

CHAPATIS

9 oz (250 g) wholewheat flour $\frac{1}{4}$ pint (150 ml) water
1$\frac{1}{2}$ teaspoons oil *or* ghee

SERVES 4

Put the wholewheat flour into a bowl with the oil or ghee and the water, and mix them to a firm dough, then knead the dough for 5 minutes. Cover with a damp cloth and leave to rest for a couple of hours, then knead the dough again for 5 minutes. Take pieces of dough about the size of a golf ball and roll each into a 5 inch (10 cm) round. Fry the rounds on both sides in an ungreased frying pan. The chapatis can be served as they are, or brushed with a little ghee or melted butter before serving.

PURIS

These puffed-up, succulent Indian breads are made from the same basic dough as the chapatis (page 196), but the rounds are made a little smaller and are deep fried.

9 oz (250 g) wholewheat flour   ¼ pint (150 ml) water
1½ teaspoons oil *or* ghee   oil for deep frying

SERVES 4

Make the dough exactly as described for chapatis, then take pieces of dough about the size of a walnut and roll each into a circle about 3 inches (7.5 cm) diameter. Plunge one of these rounds into really hot, deep oil and fry until golden on the underside, then, using a perforated spoon, turn it over and press it down below the surface of the oil with the spoon. As you do this it will swell up. Lift the puffed-up puri out of the oil and drain on kitchen paper. Fry the remainder in the same way, three or four at a time. Keep the finished puris warm while you make the rest, then serve them immediately.

BEAN PAËLLA

Don't be put off by the rather long list of ingredients in this recipe; it's very easy to make and tastes delicious.

4 oz (125 g) beans – red kidney beans look nice, or a mixture
1 small aubergine, diced
8 oz (225 g) long grain brown rice
¾ pint (400 ml) water
½ teaspoon turmeric
2 tablespoons oil
1 large onion, peeled and chopped
1 green pepper, de-seeded and chopped
1 stick celery, chopped
2 large carrots, scraped and diced
1 large clove garlic, crushed
2 large tomatoes, peeled and chopped (you can use canned ones)
4 oz (125 g) button mushrooms, wiped and sliced
sea salt
freshly ground black pepper
2 tablespoons chopped parsley

SERVES 4

Wash, soak and rinse the beans, then cook them as usual until tender and drain them. Sprinkle the aubergine with sea salt and leave it for 30 minutes to draw out the bitter juices, then rinse and pat dry on kitchen paper. Meanwhile, wash the rice and put it into a large saucepan with the water, turmeric and sea salt. Bring it up to the boil, then give it a stir, put a lid on the saucepan and turn down the heat. Let the rice cook gently for 30 minutes.

Heat the oil in a saucepan and fry the prepared onion, pepper, celery, carrots, aubergine and garlic for 10 minutes, but don't let them brown, then add the tomatoes and mushrooms and cook for a further 5 minutes. Tip all this mixture on top of the rice and add the beans as well, then put a lid on the saucepan and let it all go on cooking over a low heat for a further 15 minutes. Then turn off the heat and leave the paella to stand for another 10 minutes. After this, stir the mixture carefully with a fork and add some sea salt and freshly ground black pepper to taste and the chopped parsley. Reheat gently if necessary before serving.

BEAN AND WHEAT CASSEROLE

It's quite easy to get the crushed, pre-cooked wheat, called 'bulgur wheat', at health shops these days, and it makes a pleasant casserole with beans and vegetables.

12 oz (350 g) mixed beans – I generally use a mixture of split red lentils, haricot beans and continental lentils
1 large onion
1 large green pepper
3 carrots
1 large clove garlic
3 sticks celery
3 tablespoons oil
1 bayleaf

5 oz (150 g) bulgur wheat
14 oz (397 g) can tomatoes
1 tablespoon tomato purée
½ teaspoon chilli powder
sea salt
freshly ground black pepper

For the topping:
a few dried breadcrumbs
a little butter

SERVES 4

Soak, drain and rinse the beans as usual, then cover them with cold water and cook them gently until they're all tender – about 1 hour. Set oven to 375°F (190°C), mark 5.

Peel and chop the onion, de-seed and chop the pepper, scrape and slice the carrots, crush the garlic and slice the celery. Then fry them all gently in the oil with the bayleaf for about 15 minutes, but don't let them brown. Remove the bayleaf. Add the bulgur wheat, tomatoes, purée and seasonings to the mixture, together with the drained beans. Spoon the mixture into a greased shallow casserole dish and sprinkle with breadcrumbs. Dot a few small pieces of butter over the top of the casserole, then bake it for about 30 minutes. Serve with a short-cooked green vegetable or green salad.

BLACK BEANS AND RICE

In the Caribbean they call this dish of black beans against white rice 'Moors and Christians'. I'm passing on the original recipe, as it was given to me, but personally I think it tastes rather bland and needs a good pinch of chilli powder and some thyme, at the very least, to spice it up, or a well-flavoured tomato or curry sauce to serve with it.

6 oz (175 g) black beans
3 tablespoons vegetable oil
1 medium onion, peeled and chopped
1 large clove garlic, crushed
1 green pepper, de-seeded and chopped
8 oz (225 g) long grain brown rice
¾ pint (400 ml) water
1 teaspoon sea salt
freshly ground black pepper

SERVES 4

Soak the beans overnight or for several hours in plenty of water, then drain and rinse them, put them into a saucepan with a good covering of cold water and cook them gently until they're tender – about an hour. Drain them and leave on one side.

Heat the oil in a medium-sized heavy-based saucepan and fry the onion, garlic and pepper for 5 or 6 minutes, until they're beginning to soften, then stir in the rice, water, sea salt and cooked beans. Bring up to the boil, then put a lid on the saucepan, turn down the heat and leave it to cook very gently for 45 minutes, after which the rice should be tender and all the liquid absorbed. Fluff up the rice with a fork and add freshly ground black pepper and more sea salt to taste if necessary.

BUTTER BEAN AND VEGETABLE CURRY

This is a mild curry with a lovely spicy flavour. I usually serve
it with fried rice, but it's also good with plain boiled brown
rice and some mango chutney.

6 oz (175 g) butter beans
3 tablespoons oil
1 onion, peeled and chopped
1 clove garlic, crushed
1 teaspoon ground cumin
1 teaspoon turmeric
¼ teaspoon chilli powder
2 tomatoes, peeled and roughly
chopped (you can used
canned ones)
1 lb (450 g) potatoes, peeled
and cut into chunky cubes
1½ teaspoons sea salt
2 bayleaves
4 oz (125 g) frozen peas

SERVES 4

Cover the butter beans with cold water and leave them to soak
for several hours, then drain and rinse them. Put the beans
into a saucepan, cover them with their height again in cold
water and let them simmer gently until they're tender, about
1¼ hours. Then drain the beans, reserving their liquor and
making it up to ½ pint (275 ml) with extra water if necessary.

Heat the oil in a good-sized saucepan and add the onion and
garlic; fry them for 5 minutes, but don't brown them, then stir
in the spices and cook for 1 minute, before adding the tomatoes.
Let them simmer together, with a lid on the saucepan, for
about 5 minutes, then add the potatoes and mix well so that
they are coated with the spice mixture. Stir in the reserved ½
pint (275 ml) of liquid and the sea salt and bayleaves. Put a lid
on the saucepan and let everything simmer gently until the
potatoes are nearly cooked, then add the butter beans and peas
and cook for a further 5-6 minutes.

CURRIED CHICK PEAS

Chopped fresh coriander is the authentic garnish for this spicy curry – and coriander is not difficult to grow – but I find chopped parsley will substitute quite happily if necessary.

8 oz (225 g) chick peas	½ teaspoon ground cumin
3 tablespoons vegetable oil	½ teaspoon ground coriander
1 teaspoon cumin seeds	½ teaspoon garam masala
1 small onion, finely chopped	1 tablespoon chopped fresh
½ teaspoon ground ginger	coriander *or* parsley
½ teaspoon turmeric	sea salt

SERVES 3-4

Wash and pick over the chick peas and put them to soak in cold water for a few hours if possible, then drain and rinse them and put them into a saucepan with plenty of cold water. Simmer the chick peas gently for 1-1½ hours, until they're tender, then drain off and reserve the cooking liquid.

Heat the oil in a medium-sized saucepan and fry the cumin seeds for 1 minute, then add the onion, ginger, turmeric, ground cumin, ground coriander and garam masala and fry for 2 minutes, stirring all the time. Mix in the cooked chick peas and ½ pint (275 ml) of the reserved cooking liquid and bring to the boil. Put a lid on the saucepan and let everything simmer gently for 10-15 minutes. Season to taste and sprinkle with the chopped coriander or parsley; serve with plenty of brown rice and a side salad of grated carrot, banana and yoghurt, garnished with chopped walnuts.

CURRIED LENTIL AND PINEAPPLE

Many of the pulses are enhanced by being served with something sweet and I particularly like this mixture of split red lentils and pineapple. It's an English-style curry and nice with a garnish of desiccated coconut and sliced tomato. Serve it with some fluffy brown rice and lime pickle.

1 large onion
1 clove garlic
2 tablespoons oil
4 teaspoons curry powder
12 oz (350 g) split red lentils, washed
14 oz (397 g) can pineapple pieces

1½ pints (850 ml) water
sea salt
freshly ground black pepper

To serve:
a little desiccated coconut
1 tomato, sliced

SERVES 4

Peel and finely chop the onion; crush the garlic. Fry them together in the oil in a large saucepan for about 10 minutes, then mix in the curry powder and lentils and stir for a minute or two so that they get well coated with the oil and curry powder. Drain and roughly mash the pineapple and add it to the saucepan, together with the 1½ pints (850 ml) water. Bring the mixture up to the boil, then cover the saucepan with a lid and cook over a gentle heat for 20-30 minutes, until the lentils are soft. Season with sea salt and freshly ground black pepper. Pile on a warm serving dish, sprinkle with the desiccated coconut and garnish with the sliced tomato.

CURRIED MUNG DAL

Whether or not you soak the mung beans is up to you; they cook quickly in any case.

12 oz (350 g) mung beans	1½ teaspoons ground cumin
4 tablespoons oil	1½ teaspoons turmeric
1 large onion, peeled and chopped	½-1 teaspoon chilli powder
	sea salt
1 large clove garlic, crushed	freshly ground black pepper

SERVES 4

Soak, drain and rinse the beans, cover them with cold water and cook in the usual way until tender – 20-30 minutes. Or cook the beans without soaking, in which case they will take around 30-40 minutes to soften. Drain off any extra water.

Heat the oil in a medium-sized saucepan and fry the onion and garlic for 10 minutes, then add the cumin, turmeric and chilli powder and cook for a further 2-3 minutes. Stir in the drained mung beans and season well with sea salt and freshly ground black pepper. Cook the mixture over a low heat, stirring all the time, until everything is well blended and piping hot. Serve with cooked brown rice and a side salad – apple, celery and yoghurt, perhaps.

CURRIED RED KIDNEY BEANS

The addition of fresh ginger gives this curry a lovely spicy flavour. To prepare the fresh ginger, which looks like a gnarled brown root, simply peel and then finely grate it – see page 48. If you can't get any, you can use ground ginger instead.

8 oz (225 g) red kidney beans, soaked, drained and rinsed
1 medium-sized onion
1 large clove garlic
1½ tablespoons vegetable oil
1-2 teaspoons grated fresh ginger
2 teaspoons ground coriander

1 teaspoon turmeric
½ teaspoon ground cumin
½ teaspoon garam masala
2 large tomatoes, peeled and chopped (you can use canned ones)
sea salt

SERVES 4

Cover the red beans with plenty of water and cook until tender. Peel and chop the onion and crush the garlic; fry them in the oil in a largish saucepan, together with the grated ginger, for 6-7 minutes, stirring them from time to time, then add the ground coriander, turmeric and garam masala and cook for a further minute or two, stirring, before adding the tomatoes. Then put a lid on the saucepan and let everything cook gently for 5 minutes.

Drain the cooked beans, reserving ¼ pint (150 ml) of the liquid, and add this to the tomato and spice mixture, together with a good teaspoon of sea salt. Let it simmer for a further 5 minutes, then add the drained beans and heat them through. Serve with some fluffy boiled brown rice and chutney.

DAL

As the split red lentils used in this recipe cook in half an hour without soaking, this dish is quickly made. In fact if you want to serve it with brown rice, it's best to get the rice cooking before you start making the dal.

8 oz (225 g) split red lentils
¾ pint (400 ml) water
1 bayleaf
3 tablespoons oil
1 large onion, peeled and chopped
1 clove garlic, crushed
1 teaspoon turmeric
1 teaspoon ground cumin
1 teaspoon ground coriander
½ teaspoon ground ginger
2 tomatoes, skinned and chopped
1 large carrot, scraped and diced
1 large green pepper, deseeded and sliced
1 leek, washed and sliced
sea salt
freshly ground black pepper

SERVES 3-4

Put the lentils, water and bayleaf into a saucepan and cook gently for about 30 minutes, until the lentils are tender and have absorbed all the water.

Meanwhile, heat the oil in a saucepan and fry the onion and garlic with the turmeric, cumin, coriander and ginger for 10 minutes, stirring from time to time, then add the tomatoes and cook for a further minute or two before putting in the carrot, pepper and leek. Mix well, so that all the vegetables are coated with the spices, then put a lid on the saucepan, turn down the heat and cook gently for about 15 minutes or until the vegetables are all tender. Stir the vegetables into the cooked lentils; season with sea salt and freshly ground black pepper and serve with plain boiled or fried brown rice.

JAPANESE RED-COOKED RICE

'Sekihan', as this dish is called, is known as a happy food in Japan because it turns out a pinkish red and the Japanese consider that colour to be lucky and joyous. For this reason, it is traditional to serve 'sekihan' at festivals and, in particular, at weddings.

If you wanted to be really authentic you'd use a Japanese rice for this recipe. I find a short grain brown rice is quite satisfactory, although of course the red colouring is not quite so intense.

You need to start this dish at least a day before you plan to eat it.

4 oz (125 g) adzuki beans
8 oz (225 g) short grain brown rice

sea salt
1-2 teaspoons black sesame seeds

SERVES 3-4

Wash the adzuki beans, put them into a saucepan, and cover them with 2 pints (1.3 l) of water. Simmer the beans for about 40-45 minutes, until they're tender, then drain them well, reserving the liquid.

Wash and pick over the rice; put it into a bowl and pour in the reserved bean liquid. Leave in a cool place to soak overnight.

Next day, drain the rice (the liquid will not be needed any more). Mix the cooked adzuki beans with the rice, also a little sea salt, and place them in the top of a steamer. Steam the rice and beans gently for 40-60 minutes, until the rice is tender.

Heat the sesame seeds in a dry frying pan for 2-3 minutes,

until they're lightly toasted, then mix them with ½ teaspoon of sea salt. Serve the rice sprinkled with the sesame seeds and hand round soy sauce (preferably Japanese).

A crunchy green salad, with a flavoursome, slightly sweet dressing, goes well with this.

KHITCHARI

Khitchari is a mixture of rice and mung beans and the name actually means 'mess', as in 'mess of pottage' and is the origin of 'kedgeree'. It's a deliciously spicy mixture and the only accompaniment it needs is some mango chutney and perhaps a side salad of sliced tomato and raw onion rings.

8 oz (225 g) mung beans
8 oz (225 g) long grain brown
  rice
1 large onion
3 tablespoons oil
4 cloves garlic, crushed
½ teaspoon turmeric powder
½ teaspoon ground ginger
½ teaspoon garam masala

1 teaspoon ground cumin
pinch of chilli powder
3 tomatoes, peeled
1 large potato, peeled and cut
  into chunky pieces
1½ pints (850 ml) water
2 tablespoons lemon juice
sea salt

SERVES 3-4

Wash and pick over the beans and the rice. Peel and chop the onion and fry it in the oil in a medium-sized saucepan for 5 minutes, then add the garlic, turmeric, ginger, garam masala, cumin and chilli powder, and fry for a further 3-4 minutes, stirring from time to time. Quarter two of the tomatoes (reserve the other for garnish) and add to the saucepan, together with the potato, mung beans and rice. Fry over a gentle heat for 5 minutes, then stir in the water. Bring the mixture up to the boil, then cover the saucepan, turn down the heat and cook very gently for about 45 minutes, until the rice and beans are cooked. Turn off the heat and leave the saucepan to stand, covered, for a further 10-15 minutes, by which time all the liquid should have been absorbed. Add lemon juice and sea salt to taste, stirring the mixture gently with a fork to avoid mashing the rice. Serve garnished with the remaining tomato, cut into rings.

If you want to make a spicier version, a few cardamom pods, 4 or 5 cloves or a small piece of cinnamon stick can be added with the other spices.

QUICK LENTIL CURRY

This is a simple, English-style curry; serve it with some nice nutty brown rice and plenty of mango chutney.

2 onions, peeled and chopped
1 apple, peeled and chopped
3 tablespoons oil
1 bayleaf
1 large clove garlic, crushed
1-1½ tablespoons curry powder

12 oz (350 g) split red lentils, washed but not soaked
1½ pints (850 ml) water
sea salt
freshly ground black pepper
a little lemon juice to taste

SERVES 4

Fry the onion and apple in the oil in a medium-sized saucepan for 5 minutes, then add the bayleaf, garlic and curry powder and continue to cook for a further 3-4 minutes. Stir in the lentils and mix them round so that they get coated in the oil and curry powder, then add the water and bring the mixture up to the boil. Put a lid on the saucepan, turn the heat down and leave the mixture to simmer gently for about 30 minutes, or until the lentils are cooked. Season with sea salt, freshly ground black pepper, and lemon juice; remove bayleaf before serving.

RICE WITH CHICK PEAS AND TOMATOES

This rice dish is good hot or cold and it's full of protein. I think it's worth using olive oil if possible, because of the flavour.

12 oz (350 g) chick peas
8 oz (225 g) long grain brown rice
¾ pint (400 ml) water
sea salt
2 large onions
6 tablespoons olive oil

4 cloves garlic, crushed
1 lb (450 g) tomatoes, skinned and sliced
2-3 tablespoons chopped parsley
2 tablespoons lemon juice
freshly ground black pepper

SERVES 4

Soak and cook the chick peas as usual, then drain them and mash lightly to break them up a little. Wash the rice carefully, then put it into a medium-sized saucepan with the water and 1 teaspoonful of sea salt. Bring up to the boil, then put a lid on the saucepan and leave to simmer very gently for 45 minutes to cook the rice.

Meanwhile, peel and finely chop the onions and fry them in

the olive oil in a large saucepan until they're soft but not browned – 10 minutes. Add the garlic, chick peas and tomatoes and cook for a further few minutes to make everything nice and hot, then stir in the cooked rice and the chopped parsley and lemon juice, using a fork so that you don't mash the rice. Add more sea salt to taste and a good grinding of black pepper and serve immediately, or, let the mixture cool and then serve it as part of a salad meal.

RICE AND PEAS

The 'peas' in this dish are actually red kidney beans, but this recipe was given to me by a friend who lives in the Caribbean, and I've kept the original name. She tells me it's a popular dish out there and they generally use immature or 'water coconuts', as they call them, for the coconut milk. Here, I've found the best way to make the coconut milk is to put some pieces of fresh coconut into a liquidizer, together with the liquid in the coconut (if present) and some water, blend to a purée, then strain and use the resulting liquid. Alternatively, you could melt about 4 oz (125 g) of creamed coconut (see page 46) in ¾ pint (400 ml) boiling water and use that.

2 tablespoons oil
1 medium onion, peeled and chopped
1 red pepper, de-seeded and chopped
12 oz (350 g) long grain brown rice

¾ pint (400 ml) coconut milk
½ teaspoon dried thyme
sea salt
freshly ground black pepper
½ pint (275 ml) cold water
6 oz (175 g) red kidney beans, soaked, cooked and drained

SERVES 4

Heat the oil in a large saucepan and fry the onion until golden. Add the pepper, rice, coconut milk, thyme, sea salt, freshly ground black pepper and water and bring up to the boil, then cover the saucepan, turn the heat right down and leave to cook very slowly for 45 minutes, until the rice is tender and all the liquid absorbed. Stir in the cooked red beans, using a fork so that you don't mash the rice, and cook for a further few minutes to heat the beans through. Serve with a nice crisp green salad with a herby dressing.

SIMPLE CURRIED LENTILS

This spicy lentil mixture is lovely with plain boiled brown rice and a tomato and onion or cucumber and yoghurt side salad.

8 oz (225 g) continental lentils
2 large onions, peeled and chopped
2 cloves garlic, crushed
2 oz (50 g) butter
2 teaspoons ground coriander
2 teaspoons ground cumin
juice of ½ lemon
sea salt
freshly ground black pepper

SERVES 3

If possible soak the lentils for a few hours in cold water, then rinse them and put them into a saucepan with water just to cover them; simmer them for about 40 minutes, or until they're tender. If there isn't time to soak them, either do the quick, hot soak (see page 40) and then cook them, or put the washed lentils into a saucepan with plenty of water and simmer them until they're tender – about 1¼ hours or so. In any case, drain the lentils well.

Fry the onion and garlic in the butter for about 5 minutes, then add the ground coriander and cumin and cook for a further 5 minutes. Stir the onion and spices into the cooked lentils and flavour with the lemon juice, sea salt and freshly ground black pepper.

That's the basic, simple curry, but you can jazz it up by adding other vegetables such as sliced green pepper or button mushrooms; simply fry them with the onions.

SOYA BEAN CURRY

You need to allow time for the soya beans to soak and cook, so it's a good idea to get started on this recipe a day or two before you plan to make it – the cooked soya beans can always wait in the refrigerator, if necessary!

6 oz (175 g) soya beans	¾ pint (400 ml) water
1 large onion	4 oz (125 g) sultanas
1 clove garlic	sea salt
1 dessert apple	freshly ground black pepper
2 tablespoons oil	lemon juice
2-3 teaspoons curry powder	a little sugar
2 tablespoons flour	

SERVES 4

Wash the soya beans, cover them with plenty of cold water and leave them to soak for 12 hours. Then drain and rinse them thoroughly and put them into a saucepan with a good covering of water. Cook them gently until they're very tender – this takes about 4 hours. Drain the beans.

Peel and chop the onion, crush the garlic; peel, core and chop the apple and fry them in the oil for 10 minutes, without browning, then stir in the curry powder and flour and cook for a minute or two longer. Pour in the water and stir until thickened, then add the sultanas and soya beans and simmer gently, covered, for 15 minutes. Season with sea salt and freshly ground black pepper and add a little lemon juice and if necessary a dash of sugar to taste.

This is good served with plain boiled rice and some mango chutney.

SPLIT PEA DAL WITH HARDBOILED EGGS

This is a pretty dish, yellow split pea dal against white and yellow hardboiled eggs with a garnish of fresh green parsley. It's nice with plain fluffy brown rice.

8 oz (225 g) yellow split peas
4 tablespoons vegetable oil
2 large onions, peeled and chopped
2 large cloves garlic, crushed
3 teaspoons ground cumin
3 teaspoons turmeric
1 tablespoon lemon juice
sea salt
freshly ground black pepper
4 hardboiled eggs, cut into quarters
1-2 tablespoons chopped parsley

SERVES 4

Soak the split peas in cold water for several hours, then rinse them and cook them in fresh cold water until they're tender.

Drain off any excess liquid.

Meanwhile, heat the vegetable oil in a good-sized saucepan and fry the onion and garlic for 5 minutes, then add the ground cumin and turmeric and fry for a further 5 minutes. Mix in the cooked split peas and heat gently, stirring often to prevent sticking. When it's piping hot, add the lemon juice and sea salt and freshly ground black pepper to taste and serve it heaped up on a warm serving dish with the hardboiled egg quarters round the edge and the parsley sprinkled on top.

WEST INDIAN RED BEANS

The creamed coconut in this recipe gives the touch of sweetness so characteristic of Caribbean cookery. It also thickens the sauce. You should be able to buy it at a health shop; see page 46.

Incidentally, this dish is always very strongly seasoned with thyme, but if you think the amount given will be too powerful, start with less. West Indian red beans are nice served with lots of plain boiled brown rice.

8 oz (225 g) red kidney beans
1 large onion, peeled and sliced
1 large carrot, scraped and sliced

1 large clove garlic, crushed
1 tablespoon dried thyme
3 oz (75 g) creamed coconut
sea salt
freshly ground black pepper

SERVES 4

Soak the beans for several hours in cold water, then drain and rinse them. Put the beans, onion, carrot and garlic into a large saucepan and cover them with cold water; simmer gently for

45 minutes, until the beans are nearly cooked, then add the thyme and continue cooking for another 15-30 minutes to finish cooking the beans. Cut the creamed coconut into pieces and add to the bean mixture; heat gently, stirring occasionally, until all the creamed coconut has melted. Season carefully with sea salt and freshly ground black pepper.

Stuffed Vegetables

I'm particularly fond of stuffed vegetables because it's possible to make them look so colourful and attractive. And although many of these dishes are really quite cheap, they always look that little bit special.

You may feel that these stuffed vegetables are rather fiddly and time-consuming to prepare, but as with most pulse cookery, they're done in simple stages and it's largely a question of organization. I find that if I know in advance what I'm going to cook it makes all the difference and I can fit in a lot of the preparation around other jobs – putting the pulses to soak in the evening while I'm waiting for the kettle to boil, letting them simmer while I'm getting breakfast next morning, for instance, so they're all ready when I want to use them.

The stuffings all freeze well, so if you've got a freezer it's worthwhile making up an extra amount ready for another occasion.

AUBERGINES STUFFED WITH CHICK PEAS

This is a lovely mixture, reminiscent of Middle Eastern dishes. It's good served cold, as well as hot.

2 medium-sized aubergines
sea salt
oil

For the stuffing:
1 large onion, peeled and sliced
1 large clove garlic, crushed
3 tablespoons oil

3 large tomatoes, skinned and chopped
6 oz (175 g) chick peas, soaked, cooked and drained
2-3 teaspoons lemon juice
2 good tablespoons chopped parsley
freshly ground black pepper

SERVES 4

Cut the aubergines in half and scoop out the insides. Sprinkle the insides of the aubergine skins and the scooped-out flesh with sea salt and leave on one side for about 30 minutes for the bitter juices to be drawn out. Then wash the aubergine and pat dry.

Set the oven to 350°F (180°C), mark 4. Put a little oil in the base of a frying pan and fry the aubergine skins on both sides to soften them a little, then place them in an oiled shallow casserole dish. Fry the onion, garlic and scooped-out aubergine flesh in 3 tablespoons of oil in a large saucepan until they're tender – about 10 minutes – then add the tomatoes and cook for a further 2-3 minutes. Remove from the heat and add the drained chick peas, lemon juice, parsley and sea salt and freshly ground black pepper to taste. Divide the mixture between the aubergine skins, piling it up well. Bake the aubergines in the oven for 30-40 minutes. They're nice with creamy mashed potatoes and a cooked green vegetable.

AUBERGINES STUFFED WITH CONTINENTAL LENTILS AND MUSHROOMS

Serve some complementary protein with this dish to take full advantage of the pulse protein: buttered rice, perhaps, or a yoghurt and cucumber starter, or cheesecake for dessert.

2 medium-sized aubergines
sea salt
oil

For the stuffing:
1 large onion, peeled and chopped
2 cloves garlic, crushed
3 tablespoons oil
4 oz (125 g) button mushrooms, wiped and sliced

4 oz (125 g) continental lentils, soaked and cooked as usual
1-2 teaspoons lemon juice
2 tablespoons chopped parsley
freshly ground black pepper

To finish:
a few dried crumbs
a little grated cheese

SERVES 4

Prepare the aubergines as described in the previous recipe, salting them then frying the skins in oil. Arrange the skins in a shallow casserole.

Set the oven to 350°F (180°C), mark 4. Fry the onion, garlic and scooped-out aubergine flesh in 3 tablespoons of oil in a good-sized saucepan for about 10 minutes, until the onion is soft, then add the mushrooms and cook for a further 4-5 minutes. Mix in the lentils, lemon juice, parsley and some sea salt and freshly ground black pepper to taste. Pile the mixture into the aubergine skins and sprinkle with some crumbs and grated cheese. Bake them in the oven for 30-40 minutes, until the skins are completely cooked and the topping a nice golden brown.

COURGETTES WITH CHICK PEA AND MUSHROOM STUFFING

Chick peas are used a lot in stuffed vegetable dishes in the Middle East. In this recipe I think their firm texture contrasts well with the tender courgette and mushrooms.

4 good-sized courgettes, about 1½ lb (700 g) altogether

For the stuffing:
4 oz (125 g) chick peas
2 oz (50 g) butter
1 onion, peeled and chopped
2 cloves garlic, crushed

4 oz button mushrooms, wiped and sliced
1-2 teaspoons ground coriander
juice of ½ lemon
2 tablespoons chopped parsley
sea salt
freshly ground black pepper

SERVES 4

Soak, drain, rinse and cook the chick peas as usual. Set the oven to 350°F (180°C), mark 4. Wash the courgettes, then cut them in half lengthwise and scoop out the insides, leaving a 'shell'. Arrange these in a buttered shallow casserole dish Chop up the scooped-out courgette. Melt the butter in a saucepan and fry the onion and garlic for 5 minutes, then add the chopped courgette and the sliced mushrooms and cook for a further 5 minutes. Mix in the ground coriander, the drained chick peas, lemon juice and parsley. Season with sea salt and freshly ground black pepper and pile the mixture into the courgette 'shells'. Bake them in the oven for 30-40 minutes, until the courgettes are tender. They're nice served with a tomato sauce and some French beans, or, Middle Eastern style, chilled, with natural yoghurt.

MARROW WITH RED KIDNEY BEAN STUFFING

The red stuffing looks attractive against the green and white marrow. I think a cheese or parsley sauce goes well with this dish

1 medium-sized tender marrow

For the stuffing:
1 large onion, peeled and chopped
1 clove garlic, crushed
2 tablespoons cooking oil
3 tomatoes, skinned and chopped
1 tablespoon tomato purée
8 oz (225 g) red kidney beans, soaked, cooked and drained
freshly ground black pepper
sea salt
½ teaspoon cinnamon

To finish:
a few crisp breadcrumbs
a little butter

To serve:
fresh parsley sprigs

SERVES 4-6

Preheat the oven to 400°F (200°C), mark 6. Wash the marrow and cut off the stem. Cut the marrow in half lengthwise and scoop out and discard the seeds. If the marrow is a bit on the tough side, or if you want to speed up the cooking time, you can par-cook it in boiling, salted water for 5 minutes, then drain it well. This is not necessary if the marrow is young and tender. Put the marrow halves into a greased shallow baking dish.

Next, make the red kidney bean mixture. Fry the onion and garlic in the oil in a largish saucepan for about 5 minutes, then stir in the tomatoes and tomato purée and cook for a further 5 minutes or so before adding the red kidney beans, mashing them a bit with the spoon. Let the mixture simmer gently for 5-6 minutes, then season it with freshly ground black pepper, sea salt and cinnamon and spoon it carefully into the two marrow halves, sprinkle with breadcrumbs, dot with a little butter and bake in the oven for about 45 minutes, or until the marrow is tender. Garnish with parsley sprigs to serve.

STUFFED MARROW

If you can get a nice tender marrow for this recipe, it won't be necessary to peel off the skin.

1 medium-sized marrow

For the stuffing:
2 oz (50 g) butter
1 large onion, peeled and chopped
2 cloves garlic, crushed
4 tomatoes, peeled and chopped (you can use canned ones)

6 oz (175 g) butter beans, soaked, cooked and drained
1 tablespoon chopped parsley
4 oz (125 g) grated cheese
sea salt
freshly ground black pepper

For the topping:
a few dried crumbs
a little butter

SERVES 4

Preheat the oven to 400°F (200°C), mark 6. Prepare the marrow as for the marrow with red kidney bean stuffing. Melt the butter and fry the onion and garlic for 10 minutes, but don't brown them, then add the tomatoes and cook for a further 3-4 minutes. Stir in the butter beans, parsley, grated cheese and sea salt and freshly ground black pepper to taste. Pile the mixture into the two marrow halves, sprinkle with crumbs and dot with a little butter. Bake in the oven for about 45 minutes, or until the marrow halves are tender and the top golden brown. This is good with buttery new potatoes and a cooked green vegetable. Spicy tomato sauce goes well with it, too.

STUFFED MUSHROOM CAPS

Those large, flat mushrooms which you can sometimes get make a very good base for a tasty lentil stuffing and look appetizing when garnished with lemon and parsley. If you serve the mushrooms on circles of fried bread, it makes them more substantial, as well as giving a pleasantly crisp texture. (Incidentally, if you cut the circles for the fried bread first, the excess bread can be made into crumbs for the stuffing.)

12 large, flat mushrooms
vegetable oil

For the stuffing:
6 oz (175 g) continental lentils
1 large onion, peeled and chopped
1 large clove garlic, crushed
6 oz (175 g) wholewheat breadcrumbs
1 teaspoon thyme

1 tablespoon chopped parsley
grated rind and juice of half a lemon
sea salt
freshly ground black pepper
12 slices wholewheat bread

To finish:
12 slices of lemon
12 sprigs of parsley

SERVES 4-6

Wash, soak, rinse and cook the lentils as usual; drain them well. Set oven to 350°F (180°C), mark 4.

Wash the mushrooms and trim off any stalks level with the base. Chop up the stalks. Cover the base of a large saucepan with a thin layer of oil and heat it up. Then fry the mushroom caps for a minute or two on each side; remove them from the saucepan and put them on one side while you make the filling.

Put a little more oil in the saucepan (there should be about 6 tablespoons in all) and fry the onion, garlic and chopped mushroom stalks for 10 minutes, letting them brown lightly. Then mix in the wholewheat breadcrumbs and stir over the heat until they're brown and crunchy. Remove from the heat and add the lentils, thyme, parsley, grated lemon rind and enough of the juice to give a pleasant flavour. Season with sea salt and freshly ground black pepper.

Cut the slices of bread into circles to fit the mushroom caps. Fry the bread on both sides in a little oil until crisp. Arrange the bread circles on a flat ovenproof plate or baking tray and place a mushroom cap, black side up, on each. Divide the stuffing mixture between the mushroom caps, piling it up neatly. Bake them in the oven for about 20 minutes to heat them through. Decorate each with a slice of lemon and a sprig of parsley before serving. They go well with very light, creamy mashed potatoes, a simply cooked green vegetable such as French beans, and grilled tomatoes.

STUFFED ONIONS

This is a warming, winter dish and goes well with Bircher potatoes which you can cook in the oven at the same time as the onions. To make these, simply scrub some medium-sized old potatoes, halve them lengthwise and put them, cut side down, on an oiled baking sheet. Sprinkle them with sea salt (and a few caraway seeds if you like them) and bake the potatoes at the top of the oven while the onions cook in the middle.

4 large onions

For the stuffing:
3 oz (75 g) continental lentils,
   soaked and cooked as usual
1 clove garlic, crushed

2 teaspoons tomato purée
4 oz (125 g) grated cheese
½ teaspoon dried thyme
sea salt
freshly ground black pepper

SERVES 4

Peel the onions and cook them for 15 minutes in boiling salted water; drain and cool. Preheat the oven to 400°F (200°C), mark 6. With a sharp knife scoop out the inside of the onions, leaving the outer layers intact. Chop up the scooped-out onion and mix it with the cooked continental lentils, the garlic, tomato purée, cheese and thyme. Season with sea salt and freshly ground black pepper. Divide the mixture between the onions, pushing it well down into the cavities. Put the onions into an oiled ovenproof casserole and, if there's any of the stuffing mixture left over, scatter that round the onions. Bake them in the preheated oven for 30-40 minutes.

STUFFED PEPPERS

Stuffed peppers always seem to be popular. In this recipe I've suggested four medium-sized peppers, but you could use two large ones split in half.

4 medium-sized green peppers

For the stuffing:
4 oz (12 g) red kidney beans
3 oz (75 g) long grain brown
  rice, washed
½ pint (275 ml) water
1 large onion, peeled and
  chopped

1 large clove garlic, crushed
2 tablespoons oil
2 tomatoes, peeled and chopped
2 oz (50 g) walnuts, chopped
¼–½ teaspoon chilli powder
sea salt
freshly ground black pepper

SERVES 4

Wash and soak the red kidney beans as usual, then drain and
rinse them and put them into a heavy-based saucepan with the
water and simmer for 15 minutes. Add the brown rice, bring
up to the boil, then turn the heat down and leave them to
simmer gently, with a lid on the saucepan, for 45 minutes,
until the rice and beans are both cooked and all the water has
been absorbed.

Set the oven to 375°F (190°C), mark 5. Prepare the peppers
by slicing off their stalk ends and removing the seeds, then put
them into a large saucepan of boiling water and simmer them
gently for 2-3 minutes. Drain them well and pat them dry with
kitchen paper. Place the peppers in a greased shallow casserole
and leave them on one side while you make the filling.

Fry the onion and garlic in the oil for 5 minutes, then add the
tomatoes, the cooked rice and beans, walnuts, chilli powder
and sea salt and freshly ground black pepper to taste. Spoon the
filling into the peppers, replace the sliced-off tops as 'lids' and
bake in the oven for about 35-40 minutes, until the peppers are
completely tender. Serve them with a tasty tomato sauce and
some vegetables.

PEPPERS WITH LENTIL AND TOMATO STUFFING

In this recipe the wholewheat complements the pulse protein to give excellent nourishment. It's a tasty dish, good with creamy potatoes and buttered baby carrots.

4 medium-sized green peppers

For the stuffing:
1 large onion
2 cloves garlic
3 tablespoons oil
1 bayleaf
6 tomatoes, skinned and chopped *or* a 14 oz (397 g) can, well drained
6 oz (175 g) continental

lentils, soaked, cooked and drained
4 oz (125 g) wholewheat breadcrumbs
2 tablespoons chopped parsley
freshly ground black pepper
sea salt

To finish:
a little grated cheese

SERVES 4

Preheat the oven to 350°F (180°C), mark 4. Slice the tops off the peppers and remove the seeds; rinse the peppers inside and out under cold water, then put them into a large saucepan of boiling, salted water and simmer them for 2-3 minutes; drain and dry them and place them in a shallow greased casserole.

Peel and slice the onion and crush the garlic; fry them together in the oil with the bayleaf for 10 minutes, then remove the bayleaf and stir in the tomatoes, lentils, wholewheat breadcrumbs, parsley and a good seasoning of freshly ground black pepper and sea salt. Mix it all together well, then divide it between the four peppers, piling them up well.

Sprinkle the tops with grated cheese and bake them in the oven for 30-40 minutes, or until the peppers are tender.

STUFFED TOMATOES (HOT)

Served on crisp circles of fried bread these make an excellent starter, or, with brown rice or buttered noodles and a green vegetable or salad, they're excellent for a main meal.

8 large tomatoes
sea salt

2 teaspoons dried basil
freshly ground black pepper
2 tablespoons lemon juice

For the stuffing:
2 large onions, peeled and chopped
3 cloves garlic, crushed
8 tablespoons olive oil
12 oz (350 g) chick peas, cooked and drained

To serve:
fresh parsley sprigs
8 circles of fried bread, if serving the tomatoes as a starter

SERVES 8 AS A STARTER OR 4 AS A MAIN DISH

Cut a small slice from the top of each tomato, then, using a teaspoon, carefully scoop out the inside – this will not be needed in the recipe but can be used in tomato soups and sauces, etc. Sprinkle the insides of the tomatoes with a little sea salt; place the tomatoes upside down on a plate and leave for 30 minutes to draw out any excess liquid.

Preheat the oven to 350°F (180°C), mark 4. Fry the onions and garlic in 3 tablespoons of the olive oil in a medium-sized saucepan for 10 minutes, until soft but not browned, then mix in the cooked chick peas, mashing them a bit as you do so. Add the basil, some sea salt and freshly ground black pepper and the lemon juice.

Use a little of the remaining olive oil to grease a shallow ovenproof dish. Place the tomatoes in the dish and fill each with some of the chick pea mixture, piling it up well. Put any remaining mixture around the edges of the dish. Replace the sliced-off tomato tops as 'lids'. Pour the remaining oil over the tops of the tomatoes and bake them in the oven for 30-40 minutes. Serve them from the dish, garnished with some fresh parsley sprigs. Or, if serving them as a starter, place each tomato on a circle of crisp fried bread and serve on individual plates.

STUFFED TOMATOES (COLD)

Flageolet beans make an attractive filling for stuffed tomatoes, their pale green colour contrasting well with the red.

4 large, firm tomatoes
sea salt

1 tablespoon chopped parsley
freshly ground black pepper
1-2 drops tabasco

For the stuffing:
4 oz (125 g) flageolet beans
4 tablespoons mayonnaise
1 tablespoon chopped chives

To serve:
a few crisp lettuce leaves
parsley sprigs

SERVES 4

Soak, drain, rinse and cook the beans as usual; drain well and mash them roughly.

Halve the tomatoes and scoop out their centres – these will

not be needed for this recipe. Sprinkle the insides of the tomatoes with sea salt and then put them upside down on a plate to drain off any excess liquid.

Mix together the beans, mayonnaise, chives and parsley. Season with sea salt and freshly ground black pepper and one or two drops of tabasco. Fill the tomato cavities with the bean mixture and chill. To serve them, place the tomatoes on a base of crisp lettuce leaves and garnish with the parsley.

TOMATOES STUFFED WITH CHICK PEAS (COLD)

This makes a lovely starter or it can be served as the centre-piece of a light salad meal, on crisp lettuce leaves, accompanied by thin brown bread and butter.

4 good-sized tomatoes
sea salt

For the stuffing:
1 clove garlic
2 tablespoons mayonnaise
2 tablespoons natural yoghurt
4 oz (125 g) chick peas, cooked

and drained
1 teaspoon chopped fresh basil *or* ½ teaspoon dried basil
1 tablespoon chopped parsley
freshly ground black pepper
crisp lettuce leaves

SERVES 4

Slice the tops off the tomatoes and scoop out the seeds – these will not be needed. Sprinkle the insides of the tomatoes with sea salt and leave them upside down on a plate for about 30 minutes for the excess liquid to drain away. Meanwhile, crush the garlic and mix it with the mayonnaise, yoghurt, chick peas and herbs; season to taste with sea salt and freshly ground black pepper.

Fill each of the tomatoes with some of the chick pea mixture and arrange them on a base of crisp lettuce leaves to serve. If you like, you can replace the sliced-off tops of the tomatoes as 'lids', with the creamy chick pea mixture peeping out underneath them.

Top-of-the-cooker Dishes

One of the complaints my friends make about pulse cookery is that you've got to be so organized with all the soaking and long cooking. It's no good, they say, for the quick meals they so often have to prepare. Frankly I think some of this is psychological: if you're determined enough to want to use pulses, or poor enough to have to, you jolly well make sure you remember to put them to soak, and the actual cooking is most undemanding and can be going on quietly while you get on with other things. But having said this, I do sympathize; and in this section I've included some recipes which can be made very quickly. Indeed, with a pressure cooker, all the recipes in this section can be made fairly quickly, using the quick-soak method described on page 40, followed by a short cooking period at 15 lbs pressure. And in Appendix 2 on page 279, I've listed the recipes throughout the book which can be speedily made by using canned beans instead of dried.

Some cooked pulses stowed away in the refrigerator or deep freeze are also helpful for reducing preparation time, whilst in thoroughly disorganized, hectic periods, tinned butter beans, red kidney beans, chick peas or continental lentils (which you can sometimes get at specialist food shops) can be used for extra quick and speedy results.

BEAN RATATOUILLE

The addition of some beans to ratatouille turns this delectable dish into a main meal, and if you use rather bland beans, such as haricot or cannellini, they will soak up the lovely flavour of olive oil and garlic.

6 oz (175 g) haricot beans
1 lb (450 g) courgettes
1 lb (450 g) aubergines
sea salt
2 large onions, peeled and chopped
3 tablespoons olive oil
3 tablespoons vegetable oil

3 large cloves garlic, crushed
2 red peppers, de-seeded and chopped
4 tomatoes, skinned and chopped (you can use canned ones)
freshly ground black pepper
a little chopped parsley

SERVES 4

Soak, rinse and cook the beans as usual until they're tender, then drain them. Cut the courgettes and aubergines into small dice and put them into a colander with a good sprinkling of sea salt. Place a plate with a weight on it on top and leave for at least half an hour for any bitter liquids to be drawn out of the aubergines and excess moisture out of the courgettes. Rinse them and pat dry.

Fry the onion in the oils in a large saucepan for about 10 minutes, then add the garlic, peppers and the courgettes and aubergines. Cook gently with a lid on the saucepan for about 30 minutes, then add the tomatoes and cook for a further 30 minutes. Then stir in the beans and allow them to heat through. Season the mixture with sea salt and freshly ground black pepper and sprinkle it with parsley just before serving.

I like this with hot garlic bread, which, of course, supplies cereal protein to complement the beans and provide first-class nourishment. With a green salad, fragrant with fresh herbs and a glass of chilled wine, bean ratatouille makes a lovely summer supper.

BEANS WITH MARROW AND CORN

For this Latin American dish you can use any white beans; I like it with black eyed beans, but haricot or cannellini beans are also good. Choose if possible a marrow that's tender enough for the skin to be left on, as the stripey green looks attractive against the red tomato and yellow sweetcorn. Pumpkin, that very popular ingredient in Latin American cookery, can be used when in season, but this of course needs the skin removing.

3 tablespoons olive oil
1 large onion, peeled and chopped
1 large clove garlic, crushed
14 oz (397 g) can tomatoes
1 teaspoon dried basil
1 teaspoon dried oregano
8 oz (225 g) black eyed beans, soaked and cooked until very nearly tender
1 lb (450 g) marrow, cut into largish dice
4 oz (125 g) sweetcorn kernels
sea salt
freshly ground black pepper

SERVES 4

Heat the oil in a good-sized saucepan and fry the onion for 5 minutes, until beginning to soften, then add the garlic, tomatoes, basil and oregano, and cook fairly fast for about 10 minutes, without a lid on the saucepan, to make a thickish sauce. Stir in the drained beans and marrow and simmer gently for about 10 minutes, until the marrow is nearly cooked, then mix in the sweetcorn and continue to cook until everything is tender and the mixture piping hot. Season with sea salt and freshly ground black pepper and serve at once.

BEANY GOULASH

Strictly speaking, a genuine Hungarian 'gulyas' or 'goulash' doesn't contain sour cream: but then neither would it be made from beans, so if you think a dollop of sour cream would be nice with this, I reckon you can go right ahead and have one! Incidentally, if you want the best flavoured paprika pepper it's well worth looking out for a 'Hungarian' or 'rose' one, and buying only a small quantity at a time.

8 oz (225 g) cannellini or haricot beans
4 cloves garlic, crushed
1 lb (450 g) onions, peeled and sliced
4 tablespoons oil
2 large green peppers, de-seeded and sliced
2 14 oz (397 g) cans tomatoes

4 tablespoons tomato purée
2-4 teaspoons paprika
sea salt
freshly ground black pepper
a little sugar

To serve:
¼ pint (150 ml) soured cream, if liked

SERVES 4

Soak the beans in cold water for several hours, then rinse and simmer them in fresh water for about 1 hour, until they're tender. Fry the garlic and onions in the oil in a large saucepan for about 10 minutes, until the onion is soft, then add the green pepper and fry for a further 4-5 minutes. Mix in the tomatoes, tomato purée, the drained beans and paprika pepper, sea salt, freshly ground black pepper and perhaps a little sugar to taste. Simmer the mixture for about 15 minutes, without a lid on the saucepan, to make everything nice and hot and to reduce the liquid a little. Serve with the soured cream if liked.

BEORIJCH

An unusual mixture of black eyed beans and nuts, this is an Armenian dish that's rich in protein and quick to make. It's also surprisingly tasty.

8 oz (225 g) black eyed beans
1 large onion, peeled and chopped
4 tablespoons olive oil
1 clove garlic, crushed
2 tomatoes, skinned and chopped (you can use canned ones)
1 tablespoon tomato purée

4 oz (125 g) mixed nuts, roughly chopped in the liquidizer
2 tablespoons chopped fresh parsley
sea salt
freshly ground black pepper
a little sugar

SERVES 4

Soak and cook the black eyed beans as usual; drain them well. Fry the onion in the olive oil in a good-sized saucepan for 10 minutes, then stir in the garlic, tomatoes and tomato purée and cook for a further 10 minutes to make a thick purée. Add the nuts, parsley and the beans, mashing them slightly as you do so. Taste the mixture and season with sea salt, freshly ground black pepper and a dash of sugar if you think it's necessary. Put over a gentle heat for about 10 minutes, stirring often to prevent sticking. Serve piping hot, with buttered new potatoes or creamy mashed potatoes and a cooked green vegetable or crisp green salad.

BLACK EYED BEAN AND VEGETABLE STEW

This is a colourful stew, with black eyed beans peeping out of a rich red tomato sauce and a garnish of fresh green parsley. It goes well with baked or creamy mashed potatoes and some buttery spinach or green beans.

8 oz (225 g) black eyed beans	14 oz (397 g) can tomatoes
1 large onion	1 tablespoon tomato purée
3 sticks celery	2-3 tablespoons red wine if
3 carrots	possible
1 green pepper	sea salt
2 cloves garlic	freshly ground black pepper
2 oz (50 g) butter	2 tablespoons chopped parsley

SERVES 4

Soak the black eyed beans in cold water for several hours, then drain and rinse them. Put them into a saucepan, cover with cold water and simmer gently until tender, about 40 minutes. Drain the beans.

Peel and chop the onion; slice the celery thinly, scrape and dice the carrots. Remove seeds from the pepper, then slice it fairly thinly; crush the garlic. Melt the butter in a good-sized saucepan and add all the prepared vegetables; fry them gently, without browning, for about 10 minutes, then mix in the beans, tomatoes, tomato purée and the wine if you're using it. Season the mixture with sea salt and freshly ground black pepper and let it cook gently for 10-15 minutes, until all the vegetables are tender. Check seasoning. Serve sprinkled with the parsley.

BUTTER BEAN AND VEGETABLE AU GRATIN

I tend to think of this as a winter dish, made with root vegetables, but in fact there's no reason why it shouldn't work equally well with some of the tender early summer vegetables such as young carrots, courgettes and French beans.

6 oz (175 g) butter beans
$\frac{1}{4}$-$\frac{1}{2}$ pint (150-275 ml) milk
8 oz (225 g) carrots
8 oz (225 g) swede
8 oz (225 g) leeks
4 sticks celery
4 onions

1$\frac{1}{2}$ oz (40 g) butter
1$\frac{1}{2}$ oz (40 g) flour
4 oz (125 g) grated cheese
sea salt
freshly ground black pepper
wholewheat breadcrumbs

SERVES 4

Soak, rinse and cook the butter beans as usual, then drain them, reserving their liquid. Make the liquid up to $\frac{3}{4}$ pint (400 ml) with the milk.

Peel and dice the carrots and swede; clean and slice the leeks and celery; peel and slice the onions. Cook all the vegetables together in boiling salted water until they're just tender, then drain them.

Melt the butter in a good-sized saucepan and stir in the flour; when it 'froths', draw the saucepan off the heat and stir in the milk, then return the saucepan to the heat and stir until the sauce thickens. Let the sauce simmer gently for about 10 minutes, to cook the flour, then stir in half the cheese, the butter beans and cooked vegetables. Season with sea salt and freshly ground black pepper. Turn the mixture into a shallow heatproof casserole, sprinkle with the crumbs and remaining cheese and make hot and brown under the grill.

CHICK PEAS WITH GARLIC

This is my version of a Lebanese chick pea dish. It's very cheap (apart from the olive oil) and is another example of a natural marriage of two complementary proteins, pulses and cereals.

12 oz (350 g) chick peas
3 large cloves garlic, crushed
sea salt
freshly ground black pepper
a little olive oil

4 slices of stale bread

To serve:
wedges of lemon
paprika pepper

SERVES 4

Soak the chick peas, then rinse them and cook in fresh water as usual. Drain them, reserving their cooking water. Mash the chick peas or pass them through a vegetable mill; alternatively, liquidize then, adding some of their cooking water if necessary, to make a smooth, fairly thick purée. Flavour this purée with the garlic and add some sea salt, freshly ground black pepper and a couple of tablespoonfuls of olive oil to taste. Reheat the mixture and keep it warm.

Cut the stale bread into small dice and fry them in a little olive oil (or, if you want to economize, vegetable oil), until they're crisp.

Serve the chick pea purée topped with a little more olive oil and scatter the fried bread pieces on top; garnish with wedges of lemon and some paprika pepper.

COCIDO

There are many versions of this Spanish dish, containing varying quantities of meat. This is one of the more modest ones and, as a vegetarian, I prefer to make it without meat, although strictly speaking a piece of salted pork or bacon should be included – about 4-6 oz (125-175 g). Some of the more complicated cocidos are served as three courses; first the liquid is strained off, mixed with vermicelli and served as soup; then the chick peas and vegetables are removed from the saucepan for the next course, and finally the meat. This simple cocido is best served in one bowl, however, as a stew, with some bread or croûtons.

12 oz (350 g) chick peas	1 tablespoon paprika pepper
unsalted stock	bouquet garni – a couple of
3 potatoes	sprigs of parsley, a sprig of
2 onions	thyme and a bayleaf, tied
2 carrots	together
1 turnip	2 tablespoons oil
2 leeks	sea salt
1 small cabbage	freshly ground black pepper
2 cloves garlic	

SERVES 4

Soak the chick peas for several hours, then drain and rinse them. Put the chick peas into a large saucepan, cover them generously with unsalted stock and simmer them for about 1 hour, until they're almost tender. Meanwhile, peel the potatoes, and cut them into even-sized chunks; peel and slice the onions, carrots and turnip. Wash the leeks thoroughly and cut into slices; wash and quarter the cabbage and crush the garlic. Add the vegetables to the chick peas in the saucepan, together with the paprika pepper, bouquet garni, oil and a little more stock if you think it necessary. Simmer gently for a further 30 minutes or so until everything is done. Remove the bouquet garni; season the mixture with sea salt and freshly ground black pepper.

LENTILS AND SPINACH

You might think this a most unpromising combination, but it works well, and is so soothing to eat I don't wonder it was served to the Persian sick in the Middle Ages.

1 lb (450 g) spinach
8 oz (225 g) continental lentils, soaked and cooked until tender, then drained
1 onion, peeled and chopped
2 cloves garlic, crushed
1 oz (25 g) butter
good pinch each of ground cumin and ground coriander
sea salt
freshly ground black pepper
juice of ½ lemon

SERVES 4

Wash the spinach carefully by putting it into a big bowl of cold water and swishing it round, then draining it and repeating twice more. Shred it roughly, then put it into a dry saucepan and cook over a moderate heat, with a lid on the saucepan, until it's tender – about 10 minutes. Drain off the liquid which will have accumulated. Add the cooked drained lentils to the spinach and have the saucepan over a gentle heat to keep the spinach hot and heat the lentils through.

Fry the onion and garlic in the butter for 10 minutes, until tender, then stir in the spices and cook for a minute or two longer. Add this mixture to the spinach and lentils, together with sea salt and freshly ground black pepper to taste, and the lemon juice. Serve at once.

This dish looks attractive garnished with some wedges of hardboiled egg, yellow and white against bright green, but it's also very good served just as it is, perhaps with some slices of brown bread and butter.

LENTIL AND SPLIT PEA CASSEROLE

3 oz (75 g) split red lentils
3 oz (75 g) split peas
2½ pints (1.4 l) well-flavoured, but unsalted vegetable stock
1 lb (450 g) leeks
2 large onions
8 oz (225 g) parsnips

8 oz (225 g) carrots
2 oz (50 g) margarine
1 tablespoon flour
sea salt
freshly ground black pepper
4 oz (125 g) grated cheese

SERVES 4

Wash the lentils and split peas and put them into a saucepan with 1½ pints (850 ml) of the stock. Bring them to the boil, then turn the heat down and leave them to simmer gently until tender, about 30 minutes.

Meanwhile prepare the vegetables. Wash the leeks thoroughly and cut them into 1 inch (2.5 cm) slices, peel and chop the onions, peel the parsnips and carrots and cut them into chunky dice. Melt the margarine in a large flameproof casserole or saucepan and add all the vegetables; fry them for 5 minutes, stirring them often so that they all get well coated with the fat, but don't let them brown. Add the flour and mix well, then pour in the rest of the stock – 1 pint (550 ml) – and the cooked lentils and peas, together with any of their liquid. Season well with sea salt and freshly ground black pepper. Cover the saucepan and cook gently for about 30 minutes, until all the vegetables are tender. Then sprinkle the grated cheese on top and serve immediately.

FRIJOLES REFRITOS – RE-FRIED BEANS

This Latin American dish has rather a confusing name, because in fact the beans are only fried once, although they are first cooked in water, which may be how the name originated.

12 oz (350 g) red kidney beans
2 pints (1.3 l) water
3 large onions, peeled and chopped
3 cloves garlic, crushed
3 oz (75 g) vegetable margarine
¼–½ teaspoon chilli powder
14 oz (397 g) can tomatoes
sea salt

To serve:
triangles of fried bread

243

SERVES 4

Cover the beans with cold water and leave them to soak for several hours, then drain them and rinse under cold water. Put the beans into a saucepan with the 2 pints (1.3 l) of cold water, one of the chopped onions, one of the crushed cloves of garlic, a quarter of the margarine and the chilli powder. Bring them up to the boil, then simmer them gently for about 1 hour, with a lid on the saucepan, until the beans are tender and the liquid absorbed.

Now for the frying part. Melt the remaining margarine in another large saucepan and fry the rest of the onion and garlic for about 10 minutes, until the onion is soft, then add the tomatoes and simmer for 2–3 minutes. Mix the beans into the onion and tomatoes a couple of tablespoonfuls at a time, mashing them roughly as you do so. When all the beans have been added, cook the mixture gently for about 10 minutes, to heat everything through.

Traditionally this is an accompaniment for tortilla dishes. I think it needs something crisp with it, so usually serve it garnished with triangles of fried bread, or crusty garlic bread, and a short-cooked green vegetable or tossed green salad.

ROOT VEGETABLE AND LENTIL STEW

Real warming winter food, this: root vegetables with pulses, and very filling and satisfying, too. You can add whatever herbs and spices you fancy; my suggestion of ground coriander and cumin makes it spicy without being 'hot'.

3 tablespoons oil

1½ lb (700 g) mixed root vegetables – swede, parsnip, carrot, turnip – peeled and diced

2 large onions, peeled and chopped

2 sticks celery, sliced

6 oz (175 g) split red lentils

2 cloves garlic, crushed

8 oz (225 g) canned tomatoes

1¼ pints (700 ml) unsalted stock

To finish:

1 onion, peeled and chopped

1-2 teaspoons ground coriander

1-2 teaspoons ground cumin

sea salt

freshly ground black pepper

juice of ½ lemon

a little chopped parsley

SERVES 3-4

Heat the oil in a large saucepan and put in the root vegetables, two-thirds of the onion and the celery. Fry the vegetables in the oil, without browning them, for about 5 minutes, then add the lentils and garlic and cook them all gently for a further 4-5 minutes, stirring often. Mix in the tomatoes and stock, put a lid on the saucepan and leave it to simmer away gently for about 30 minutes, until all the vegetables are tender and the lentils pale golden and soft. Meanwhile, fry the extra onion in the oil for 10 minutes, then add the ground coriander and cumin and fry for a further minute or two to draw out the flavour of the spices. Stir this mixture into the cooked lentils and add sea salt and freshly ground black pepper to taste and the lemon juice. Scatter with a little chopped parsley before serving.

If you prefer to cook this in the oven, it takes about an hour towards the bottom at 400°F (200°C), mark 6.

STIR-FRIED BEAN CURD WITH CARROTS

When using bean curd in a stir-fried mixture, flavouring is all-important and that's where the Chinese are so skilled. Here the flavour is supplied by the garlic, ginger, soy sauce, bean paste, sherry and stock. It's lovely to use Chinese mushrooms if you can get them – they're available dried from Chinese grocers – but if not, ordinary mushrooms can be used instead. The bean paste can also be bought from shops selling Chinese provisions, or from health shops, where it will probably be sold under the name 'miso'. It's useful for flavouring soups, stews and casseroles, as well as Chinese-style dishes.

8 oz (225 g) carrots
4 dried Chinese mushrooms *or* 8 oz (225 g) fresh mushrooms
1 onion
2 cloves garlic
a piece of root ginger, peeled and grated to give about 2 teaspoons
2 tablespoons soy sauce
½–1 teaspoon bean paste
1 teaspoon sugar
few drops of tabasco
½ teaspoon yeast extract (such as Marmite) dissolved in 4 tablespoons boiling water
1 tablespoon sherry
½ teaspoon MSG powder
8 oz (225 g) bean curd
6 tablespoons oil

SERVES 3

Prepare the carrots by scraping them and then cutting them into thin diagonal slices. Parboil them for 4-5 minutes, until they're almost tender; drain. Soak the dried mushrooms in enough water just to cover them, then drain them and cut into narrow strips. Or, if you're using ordinary mushrooms, wash and slice them. Peel and very finely chop the onion; crush the garlic; peel and finely grate the ginger. Mix together the soy sauce, bean paste, sugar, tabasco, hot water and yeast extract, sherry and MSG. Cut the bean curd into smallish dice.

When ready to cook, heat half the oil in a wok or large frying pan and fry the garlic, ginger and onion for a few seconds, then stir in the mushrooms and carrots; cook for 30 seconds, then pour in the soy sauce mixture and cook for a couple of minutes, so that all the flavours have a chance to blend. Mix in the bean curd and stir-fry for a further 2 minutes, so that everything is hot. Serve immediately.

STIR-FRIED BEAN SPROUTS WITH MUSHROOMS, CHINESE CABBAGE AND OMELETTE STRIPS

If you serve this with boiled rice it makes a complete meal that's quick to cook. As with all Chinese-style recipes, all the preparation of the vegetables should be done in advance; the actual cooking takes only a few minutes. If you're going to serve brown rice with this dish, remember to allow time for it to cook – it will take around 45 minutes.

12 oz (350 g) bean sprouts
12 oz (350 g) Chinese cabbage
8 oz (225 g) button mushrooms
2 onions
1 clove garlic
small piece of fresh ginger (to give about 2 teaspoons when peeled and grated)
2 tablespoons soy sauce
1 teaspoon sugar

1 tablespoon sherry
½ teaspoon MSG powder
6 tablespoons oil

For omelette strips:
4 eggs
sea salt
freshly ground black pepper
a little oil *or* oil and butter, for frying

SERVES 4

Wash the bean sprouts, cabbage and mushrooms; cut the cabbage and mushrooms into even-sized slices. Peel and very finely chop the onion; crush the garlic; peel and grate the ginger. Mix together the soy sauce, sugar, sherry and MSG. Whisk the eggs with some sea salt and freshly ground black pepper; have ready a small omelette pan or frying pan for making omelette strips and a wok, large frying pan or large saucepan in which to stir-fry the vegetables.

When you're ready to cook the dish, heat the oil in the wok or other pan and fry the onion, garlic and ginger for 1 minute, stirring continuously. Add the bean sprouts, Chinese cabbage and mushrooms and stir-fry them for 2 minutes, turning them over so that everything gets coated with the oil, garlic and ginger. Pour in the soy sauce mixture, reduce the heat and cook for a further 3 minutes.

While this final cooking is going on, quickly make the omelette strips. Heat a little oil or oil and butter in the omelette pan and pour in half the egg; make an omelette by cooking the egg over a brisk heat, gently pushing the eggs towards the centre as they cook, tipping the pan so that the uncooked part runs towards the edges; turn it out flat on to a plate and cut it into long strips. Make another omelette in the same way.

Taste the cooked vegetable mixture and correct the seasoning with a little sea salt and freshly ground black pepper if necessary, then pile it into a warmed serving dish, arrange the omelette strips, lattice fashion, on top, and serve immediately with plain boiled rice.

Vegetable Dishes

As you may have gathered, pulses can stand on their own, happily playing the leading role in the meal and supplying necessary nutrients. However, they're also useful for 'stretching' other, more expensive proteins which can then be served in much smaller quantities. Pease pudding, used by generations of thrifty northern housewives to help eke out the precious Sunday joint, is an example of this, although I must admit that as a vegetarian I like to serve pease pudding with a good gravy, golden roast potatoes, mint sauce and a green vegetable!

Don't be put off serving pulses as a vegetable by memories of school dinner butter beans, all dreary beige dullness. It's surprising what a little tender loving care, plus some garlic, butter, cream and herbs can do to transform them into something far from dull.

BEANS IN LEEK SAUCE

The mixture of leeks and beans is a good one and in this recipe they combine to make a creamy, protein-rich supper dish. I think this needs something crisp to go with it – fried bread, or crunchy fried potatoes.

8 oz (225 g) haricot beans
2 leeks
2 oz (50 g) butter
2 oz (50 g) flour

½ pint (275 ml) milk
4 oz (125 g) grated cheese
sea salt
freshly ground black pepper

SERVES 3-4

Soak, cook and drain the haricot beans as usual, reserving ½ pint (275 ml) of the cooking water for the sauce. Wash the leeks thoroughly, and cut them into thin slices. Melt the butter and fry the leeks in it until they're soft and lightly browned, then stir in the flour and cook together for 1-2 minutes. Mix in the bean liquid and milk and cook until boiling, stirring constantly until the mixture is smooth and thick. Simmer very gently for 10 minutes. Add the grated cheese and beans and season to taste. Reheat the beans before serving.

BUTTER BEANS AND BEETROOT WITH HORSERADISH SAUCE

This is a wartime recipe and I find the mixture of flavours pleasant and piquant.

2 medium-sized cooked beet-roots	1 oz (25 g) butter
	1 oz (25 g) flour
4 oz (125 g) butter beans, soaked, cooked and drained	¾ pint (400 ml) milk
	3 teaspoons horseradish sauce
	sea salt
For the sauce:	freshly ground black pepper

SERVES 4

Peel and dice the beetroots and mix them with the beans. Make a sauce: melt the butter in a medium-sized saucepan and add the flour. When it froths, remove from the heat and stir in the milk. Return the saucepan to the heat and stir the sauce continuously for 2-3 minutes, until it has thickened. Then turn the heat down and leave the sauce to simmer over a low heat for 10-15 minutes, to cook the flour. Stir in the horseradish sauce and some sea salt and freshly ground black pepper to taste, then carefully mix in the beans and beetroot and continue to cook the mixture very gently until the beans and beetroot are heated through. Check seasoning, then serve immediately.

BUTTER BEANS AND MUSHROOMS

If you feel this dish is rather on the extravagant side, you could omit the cream. But on the other hand, if serving these beans means you can cut down on the amount of meat in the meal, the cream may not seem such an extravagance after all.

6 oz (175 g) butter beans	¼ pint (150 ml) double cream
8 oz (225 g) young white button mushrooms	sea salt
	freshly ground black pepper
1 oz (25 g) butter	grated nutmeg
1 tablespoon lemon juice	1 tablespoon chopped parsley

SERVES 4

Soak, drain and rinse the butter beans, then put them into a saucepan, cover with water and cook until tender. Drain and keep them warm.

Wash the mushrooms and halve or quarter them if necessary. Fry them gently in the butter in a medium-sized saucepan for 2-3 minutes until they're just tender, then stir in the butter beans, lemon juice and cream and season to taste with sea salt, freshly ground black pepper and grated nutmeg. Serve sprinkled with chopped parsley.

BUTTER BEANS WITH TOMATOES, MINT AND OLIVE OIL

This is a Greek recipe for butter beans and the result is moist, rich and flavoursome. The beans can be served as a vegetable, or with fluffy brown rice. I think they make a lovely supper dish with home-made wholewheat rolls and green salad. They're also very good cold, especially if you throw in a few black olives too.

1 lb (450 g) butter beans	2 tablespoons fresh chopped
3 large onions	mint
2 cloves garlic	sea salt
¼ pint (150 ml) olive oil	freshly ground black pepper
14 oz (397 g) can tomatoes	a little sugar

SERVES 4 AS A MAIN PROTEIN DISH, 8 AS A VEGETABLE

Cover the butter beans with a good layer of cold water and leave them to soak for several hours. Then rinse them and put them into a saucepan with fresh cold water. Bring the butter beans up to the boil and simmer them until tender, then drain them.

While all this is happening, peel the onions and chop them finely; crush the garlic. Fry the onions in the olive oil in a good-sized saucepan for 10 minutes, allowing them to brown lightly, then stir in the garlic. Chop the tomatoes and add these to the saucepan, together with the cooked beans, the mint and some sea salt and freshly ground black pepper. Let the mixture simmer gently, covered, for about 20 minutes, to allow all the flavours to blend. Taste and add more sea salt and freshly ground black pepper and a dash of sugar if you think it's necessary.

CHICK PEA PURÉE FROM GREECE

This simple Greek dish, called 'revithia yahni', can be flavoured with as much parsley and mint as you like: it can take plenty. I serve it with fried bread triangles because I think it needs something crisp – and, incidentally, this gives some cereal protein to complement that of the chick peas. Crisp, dry toast would also go well with it, and some olive oil, which people can add themselves at the table. (It's also good cold, by the way.)

1 lb (450 g) chick peas
4 large onions, peeled and chopped
3 cloves garlic, crushed
4 tablespoons olive oil
14 oz (397 g) can tomatoes
2-4 tablespoons chopped fresh parsley
2-4 tablespoons chopped fresh

mint
lemon juice
sea salt
freshly ground black pepper

To serve:
crisp triangles of fried bread
olive oil

SERVES 4-6

Cover the chick peas with cold water and leave them to soak for several hours, then drain and rinse them. Put them into a saucepan with a good covering of cold water and cook them gently until they're very tender. Then drain and purée the chick peas: this can be done by whizzing them in a liquidizer (with some of their cooking liquor, but don't make them too sloppy), or by passing them through a vegetable mill.

Fry the onions and garlic in the oil for 10 minutes, then add the tomatoes and cook for a further 5 minutes. Stir in the puréed chick peas, parsley and mint and flavour with lemon juice, sea salt and freshly ground black pepper. Put over a gentle heat until everything is nice and hot, then serve with the fried bread and hand round olive oil.

CHICK PEAS WITH PEPPER AND TOMATOES

This is a simple dish which is good served as a vegetable, or, with just a tossed green salad and some warm rolls and butter, for a simple meal, with fruit and yoghurt to follow. It's also delicious cold, particularly if you can stir in a few black olives and some extra olive oil.

8 oz (225 g) chick peas
2 large onions
2 large cloves garlic
4 tablespoons olive oil
2 green peppers
8 oz (225 g) canned tomatoes
1 tablespoon tomato purée

½ teaspoon chilli powder
sea salt
freshly ground black pepper
a little sugar to taste

To serve:
2 tablespoons chopped parsley

SERVES 4

Soak, rinse and cook the chick peas as usual, then drain them. Meanwhile peel and slice the onions and crush the garlic; fry them gently in the olive oil until they're tender, about 10 minutes. Halve the green peppers and remove the seeds, then slice the peppers thinly and add them to the onions and garlic; cook for 5 minutes, then stir in the canned tomatoes, tomato purée and chilli powder and cook gently for 10 minutes. Add the chick peas and heat through gently. Season with sea salt, freshly ground black pepper and a little sugar if you think the mixture needs it. Serve garnished with chopped parsley.

CHICK PEAS IN TOMATO SAUCE

This nice, spicy chick pea mixture is also good served with buttered pasta.

8 oz (225 g) chick peas	14 oz (397 g) can tomatoes
1 small onion	1 bayleaf
1 oz (25 g) butter	sea salt
1 clove garlic, crushed	freshly ground black pepper
4 oz (125 g) button mush-	½–1 teaspoon chilli powder
rooms, washed and sliced	a little sugar

SERVES 4

Soak and cook the chick peas as usual. When they're soft, drain them and leave them on one side while you make the sauce.

Peel and chop the onion and fry it gently in the butter in a medium-sized saucepan for 5 minutes; don't let it brown. Then stir in the garlic and mushrooms and fry for a further 5 minutes. Add the tomatoes and bayleaf and let the mixture cook over a moderate heat for 10–15 minutes, until most of the liquid has boiled away, leaving a nice thick sauce. Season with sea salt, freshly ground black pepper and chilli powder, also a dash of sugar if you think it needs it. Then mix in the chick peas and cook for a further few minutes to heat them through. Check seasoning before serving.

CHILLI RED BEANS

Red beans cooked with onion, garlic, tomatoes and chilli make a spicy and unusual vegetable dish and add protein as well as colour to the meal.

8 oz (225 g) red kidney beans
1 large onion, peeled and chopped
1 large clove garlic, crushed
2 tablespoons oil

14 oz (397 g) can tomatoes
½-1 teaspoon chilli powder
sea salt
freshly ground black pepper

SERVES 4

Soak the kidney beans in cold water for several hours, then drain and rinse them and cook in fresh water for about 1 hour, until tender.

Fry the onion and garlic in the oil in a large saucepan for 10 minutes then add the tomatoes, chilli powder and the cooked and drained beans and simmer gently for 10 minutes, to heat through and allow the flavours to blend. Season with sea salt and freshly ground black pepper.

DRIED PEAS WITH MINT AND CREAM

School peas were never like this! Don't be tempted to add bicarbonate of soda to the cooking water, by the way: it ruins the flavour and destroys some of the nutrients.

8 oz (225 g) whole dried peas	2-3 tablespoons cream
1 oz (25 g) butter	sea salt
1 small onion, peeled and chopped	freshly ground black pepper
2 tablespoons chopped mint	sugar

SERVES 4

Soak, rinse and drain the peas, then cover them with water and simmer them until they're very tender. Drain the peas but keep them warm.

Meanwhile melt the butter and fry the onion lightly until it's soft but not browned. Add the onion and butter to the peas, also the mint, cream and seasoning to taste, including a dash of sugar if you think the mixture needs it. If you want a smoother finish to the dish, the peas can be passed through a mouli-légumes before any of the other ingredients are added; I think this improves them.

HARICOT BEANS WITH CELERY

The flavours of the beans and celery go well together, but as they're very much the same colour, you do need the parsley to give colour to the dish!

6 oz (175 g) haricot beans, soaked, drained and rinsed
2 small heads of celery
1 oz (25 g) butter
sea salt

freshly ground black pepper

To serve:
2 good tablespoons chopped parsley

SERVES 4

Cover the beans with water and cook them gently until they're soft. While this is happening, wash the celery thoroughly, discarding tough outer stalks. Cut the rest into even-sized pieces and cook in boiling, salted water until they're tender. Drain the celery and the beans and mix them together; add the butter and sea salt and freshly ground black pepper. Sprinkle with chopped parsley and serve at once.

HARICOT BEANS WITH CREAM AND HERBS

I think this recipe shows how simple it is to transform plain beans into something a bit special.

8 oz (225 g) haricot or butter beans
1 oz (25 g) butter
¼ pint (150 ml) cream
2-3 teaspoons lemon juice
2 tablespoons fresh chopped

green herbs: parsley, chives, tarragon, as available
sea salt
freshly ground black pepper
grated nutmeg

SERVES 4-6

Soak and cook the beans in the usual way, then drain them and, while they're still hot, add the butter, cream, a little lemon juice to taste, and the green herbs. Season carefully with sea salt, freshly ground black pepper and nutmeg. Reheat gently, just enough to make everything nice and hot (but don't let the mixture boil) and then serve immediately.

HARICOT BEANS IN TOMATO SAUCE

This dish comes from the Provence district of France, where it is often served with lamb.

1 large onion
1-2 cloves garlic
2 tablespoons oil
14 oz (397 g) can tomatoes
8 oz (225 g) haricot beans, soaked, cooked and drained
1 teaspoon oregano

sea salt
freshly ground black pepper

To serve:
1 tablespoon freshly chopped parsley

SERVES 4-6

Peel and finely chop the onion; crush the garlic. Heat the oil in a medium-sized saucepan over a moderate heat; add the onion and garlic and cook them gently until the onion has softened but not browned, then stir in the beans and tomatoes. Bring the mixture to the boil, stirring continuously and breaking up the tomatoes as you do so. Stir in the oregano. Let the mixture simmer for about 15 minutes, without a lid on the saucepan, to reduce the liquid a bit. Then season with sea salt and freshly ground black pepper and serve sprinkled with chopped parsley.

PEASE PUDDING

8 oz (225 g) yellow split peas
1 large onion, peeled and chopped
2 oz (50 g) butter *or* margarine

1 egg
sea salt
freshly ground black pepper

SERVES 4

Soak the split peas in water for a few hours, drain and rinse them and put into a saucepan with cold water just to cover them. Simmer the split peas gently until they're tender, then drain off any excess water.

Fry the onion in the butter for about 10 minutes, until it's soft, then add it to the cooked split peas, together with the egg and sea salt and freshly ground black pepper to taste. Put the mixture into a floured pudding cloth or a greased bowl with a covering of foil and steam it for 1 hour; or spoon it into a greased casserole dish and bake it in a moderate oven, 350° F (180° C), mark 4, for about 30 minutes.

PURÉE OF FLAGEOLETS

A delicate pale green purée of flageolets is useful for serving when you want to add extra protein to the meal.

8 oz (225 g) flageolet beans
1 small onion, peeled and chopped
1 oz (25 g) butter
4-6 tablespoons single cream
sea salt

freshly ground black pepper
grated nutmeg

To serve:
1 tablespoon finely chopped parsley

SERVES 4

Soak and rinse the beans, then cover them with fresh cold water and simmer them gently until tender. Drain, reserving cooking liquid.

While the beans are cooking, fry the onion gently in the butter until it is soft but not browned – about 10 minutes.

Put the beans into the liquidizer with the single cream, onion mixture, and enough of the reserved cooking liquor (if necessary) to make a smooth purée. Alternatively, pass the beans through a vegetable mill, then mix with cream and a little cooking liquor. Season with sea salt, freshly ground black pepper and grated nutmeg. Reheat gently (don't let the mixture boil) and serve garnished with chopped parsley.

STIR-FRIED BEAN SPROUTS

Bean sprouts are an absolute boon for a quick vegetable dish because you can cook them in the Chinese style in a matter of minutes, and they're crunchy, delicious and packed with vitamins.

1 lb (450 g) bean sprouts
3 tablespoons oil
1 onion, peeled and very finely chopped
1 clove garlic, crushed
small piece of fresh ginger,

to make about 2 teaspoons when peeled and grated
1 tablespoon sherry
1 tablespoon soy sauce
1 teaspoon sugar
½ teaspoon MSG powder

SERVES 2-4

Wash and drain the bean sprouts. Heat the oil in a wok or large frying pan and fry the onion, garlic and ginger for 1 minute, stirring all the time. Then add the bean sprouts and stir them for about 2 minutes, until they're well coated with the oil and flavourings. Mix in the sherry, soy sauce, sugar and MSG; reduce the heat and cook for a further 2-3 minutes, until everything is heated through. Serve at once.

TWO BEAN VEGETABLE DISH

I like the way the French serve dried beans with fresh green beans in such dishes as pistou and aïgroissade (see soup and salad sections). It's an idea that works well in a simple vegetable dish, too, and the contrasting shades of green make this mixture attractive to the eye, as well.

6 oz (175 g) flageolet beans
1 lb (450 g) French beans
1 oz (25 g) butter
1 tablespoon chopped fresh parsley
1 tablespoon chopped summer

savory, if available, otherwise use other green herbs such as chives, tarragon or extra parsley
sea salt
freshly ground black pepper

SERVES 4

Soak, drain and rinse the flageolets, then cook them in fresh cold water until they're soft. Drain and keep them warm. Meanwhile top and tail the French beans and cut them into short lengths. Cook them in a little boiling, salted water until they're tender, then drain them and add them to the cooked flageolets, together with the butter. Check the seasoning, then add the fresh herbs just before serving.

YELLOW SPLIT PEA PURÉE WITH VEGETABLES

This recipe is from Germany, and is not unlike our pease pudding. I think some triangles of crisp, fried bread go well with it.

8 oz (225 g) yellow split peas
1 pint (550 ml) water
2 medium onions, peeled and sliced
1 medium carrot, scraped and sliced
1 small leek, cleaned and sliced
1 stick celery, sliced

good pinch of dried mint *or* marjoram
1 tablespoon lemon juice
sea salt
freshly ground black pepper
1½ oz (40 g) butter

To serve:
triangles of crisp, fried bread

SERVES 4

Soak the split peas in the water for an hour or two, then drain and rinse them and put them into a saucepan with the water, half the sliced onion and all the other vegetables and herbs and let them simmer gently until the split peas are soft and the vegetables tender – about 30 minutes. Sieve or liquidize the mixture, then season it with lemon juice, sea salt and freshly ground black pepper. Spoon the mixture into a shallow heat-proof dish. Fry the remaining onion in the butter until it's beginning to soften, then pour the onion and the butter over the top of the purée. Put the purée under a fairly hot grill until the top is slightly crusted looking and the onion very crisp and brown. (Alternatively, this can be done in the oven, if it's on, but I don't think it's worth heating it up specially.)

Appendix 1:
What to Make with Which Beans

Friends have told me that when they've bought a packet of beans they'd like to be able to look up a list of things they could make with them. So I've listed the dishes in this book under the particular bean from which they're made and I've also included other recipes which (even though another type of bean is specified in the ingredients) could also be used.

ADZUKI BEANS

APPENDIX I: WHAT TO MAKE WITH WHICH BEANS

BLACK BEANS

BLACK EYED BEANS

BORLOTTI BEANS/PINTO BEANS

BRITISH FIELD BEANS/BROAD BEANS
FUL MEDAMES BEANS

The following recipes are suitable, but I suggest that the beans should be passed through a mouli-légumes.

BROAD BEANS – see BRITISH FIELD BEANS

BUTTER BEANS/LIMA BEANS

CANNELLINI BEANS – see HARICOT BEANS

CHICK PEAS

CONTINENTAL LENTILS

FLAGEOLET BEANS

FUL MEDAMES BEANS – *see* BRITISH FIELD BEANS

HARICOT BEANS/CANNELLINI BEANS

LIMA BEANS – *see* BUTTER BEANS

MUNG BEANS

PEAS

PINTO BEANS – *see* BORLOTTI BEANS

RED KIDNEY BEANS

SPLIT RED LENTILS

SOYA BEANS

SPLIT PEAS, GREEN AND YELLOW

Appendix 2: Quick Recipes

Some of the recipes in this book can be adapted, by using canned beans, for those occasions when you want something really quick. Canned red kidney beans are easy to get and so are butter beans and 'mushy' peas, while chick peas and continental lentils can sometimes be found in delicatessens. Some recipes using split red lentils, split peas and mung beans can be made in 30-40 minutes anyway, and these I've also listed.

WITH CANNED BUTTER BEANS

WITH CANNED RED KIDNEY BEANS

WITH CANNED 'MUSHY' PEAS

WITH SPLIT RED LENTILS

WITH MUNG BEANS

WITH SPLIT PEAS

WITH CANNED CHICK PEAS

WITH CANNED CONTINENTAL LENTILS

Index